How Modernity Forgets

Why are we sometimes unable to remember events, places and objects? This concise overview explores the concept of 'forgetting', and how modern society affects our ability to remember things. It takes ideas from Frances Yates' classic work, *The Art of Memory*, which viewed memory as being dependent on the stability of place, and argues that today's world is full of change, making 'forgetting' characteristic of contemporary society. We live our lives at great speed; cities have become so enormous that they are unmemorable; consumerism has become disconnected from the labour process; urban architecture has a short lifespan; and social relationships are less clearly defined – all of which has eroded the foundations on which we build and share our memories. Providing a profound insight into the effects of modern society, this book is a must-read for anthropologists, sociologists, psychologists and philosophers, as well as anyone interested in social theory and the contemporary western world.

PAUL CONNERTON is a Research Associate in the Department of Social Anthropology at the University of Cambridge. He is also an Honorary Fellow in the Institute of Germanic and Romance Studies, University of London.

How Modernity Forgets

PAUL CONNERTON

CAMBRIDGE
UNIVERSITY PRESS

CAMBRIDGE UNIVERSITY PRESS
Cambridge, New York, Melbourne, Madrid, Cape Town, Singapore, São Paulo,
Delhi, Dubai, Tokyo

Cambridge University Press
The Edinburgh Building, Cambridge CB2 8RU, UK

Published in the United States of America by Cambridge University Press, New York

www.cambridge.org
Information on this title: www.cambridge.org/9780521745802

First published 2009
Reprinted 2010

Printed in the United Kingdom at the University Press, Cambridge

A catalogue record for this publication is available from the British Library

Library of Congress Cataloguing in Publication data
Connerton, Paul.
  How modernity forgets / Paul Connerton.
    p.   cm.
  Includes index.
  ISBN 978-0-521-76215-1 (hbk)   1. Memory–Social aspects.   2. Collective
  memory.   3. Social psychology.   I. Title.
  BF378.S65C656 2009
  153.1′25–dc22
  2009017300

ISBN 978-0-521-76215-1 hardback
ISBN 978-0-521-74580-2 paperback

To Marina Voikhanskaya

The best streets are those that can be remembered. They leave strong, long-continuing positive impressions. Thinking of a city, including one's own, one might well think of a particular street and have a desire to be there; such a street is memorable ... There is a magic to great streets. We are attracted to the best of them not because we have to go there but because we want to be there. The best are as joyful as they are utilitarian. They are entertaining and they are open to all. They permit anonymity at the same time as individual recognition. They are symbols of a community and of its history; they represent a public memory.

–Allan B. Jacobs, *Great Streets*, pp. 9–11

Contents

Acknowledgements

I wish to thank the University of Manchester for the award of
a Simon Senior Research Fellowship. I also want to thank the
Trustees of the Social Theory Fund, and the Trustees of the Royal
Literary Fund, for their support. The Institute for Germanic and
Romance Studies at the University of London and the Department of Social Anthropology at the University of Cambridge both
provided congenial contexts in which I had the opportunity to try
out some of my ideas for this book in graduate seminars. I am much
indebted to Clare Campbell, Jo Canallela, Catherine Pickstock and
Vera Skvirskaia for their help in making available to me research
material which I would otherwise have found particularly difficult
of access. Nicholas Boyle has once more proved the loyalty of his
friendship by his patience and understanding when the conversa-
tion has yet again turned to the topic of place. Peter Burke, David
Forgacs, Stephen Hugh-Jones, Michael Jackson, Iris Jean-Klein,
Jo Labanyi, Michael Minden, Yael Navaro-Yashin and Marilyn
Strathern have all read earlier versions of this text, in whole or in
part; I am deeply grateful to all of them for their helpful comments.
I wish also to thank the two anonymous readers for the Cambridge
University Press for their helpful comments on my manuscript. A
special thanks, finally, to Bobbie Coe for transforming my virtually
illegible hieroglyphics into laser-copy.

I Introduction

The topic of memory is now ubiquitous. Heritage, together with its French and German equivalents, *le patrimoine* and *die Musealisierung*, museology, ethnohistory, industrial archaeology, retrofitting, retrochic, Holocaust memorials, counter-monument, counter-memory, *lieux de mémoire*: all allude to a common constellation of interests. The shape of that constellation stands out in contrast to the way in which memory emerged as something crucial to individual identity, with its fissures and fractures, when it became a central issue in philosophical thinking with Bergson, in psychoanalytic thinking with Freud, and in autobiographical literature with Proust. At the opening of the twentieth century memory was psychologised; at the close of the century the turn was to cultural memory. For the moment the investigation of cultural memory has become a culture industry in its own right.

How can we explain the frequent discussion of and the apparently high value ascribed to memory in recent years? There can be no doubt that the accumulated repercussions of the holocaustal events of the last century have played a vital role in these current preoccupations; but I want to argue that a crucial reason, if not indeed the fundamental explanation, is that modernity has a particular problem with *forgetting*.

To say this is not to claim that modernity has a monopoly of cultural amnesia, for there are demonstrably different types of structural forgetting specific to different social formations, as anthropologists and classicists were among the first to point out when they investigated the peculiarities of transmission in preliterate societies. Nor is it to claim simply that a cloud of forgetting has descended upon the contemporary horizon; any such assertion would be patently absurd. To cite three examples only: in Central and Eastern Europe, national memories were reappropriated in the wake of 1989, and the legacy of fascism and Stalinism remains to be confronted; since the 1970s the rehabilitation of ethnic memories has been perceived in North America to be a vital part of personal identity, one of the most remarkable early signs of this recognition being the resonance accorded Maxine Hong Kingston's *Woman Warrior*; and North American Indian communities, calling for the repatriation of their artefacts, have established their own museums, sought out their own National Museum grants, and hired their own anthropologists on contract.

Yet, while forgetting has not in fact descended like an all-enveloping blanket on the contemporary world, and while different social formations prior to the onset of modernity exhibit characteristic forms of forgetting which are peculiar to themselves, it remains the case that there are types of structural forgetting which are *specific* to the culture of modernity.

A number of thinkers have suspected as much. Fredric Jameson has argued that 'our entire contemporary social system has little by little begun to lose its capacity to retain its own past'.[1] Eric Hobsbawm believes that 'the destruction of the past, or rather of the social mechanisms that link one's contemporary experience to that of earlier generations, is one of the most characteristic and eerie phenomena of the late twentieth century. Most young men and women at the century's end grow up in a sort of permanent present lacking any organic relation to the public past of the times they live in.'[2] Andreas Huyssen has pointed to 'a major and puzzling contradiction in our culture. The undisputed waning of history and historical consciousness, the lament about political, social and cultural amnesia, and the various discourses, celebratory or apocalyptic, about *posthistoire* have been accompanied in the past decade and a half by a memory boom of unprecedented proportions.'[3] Jacques Le Goff joins him in linking the valorisation of memory to cultural forgetting when he says that 'the public at large ... is obsessed by the fear of losing its memory in a kind of collective amnesia – a fear that is awkwardly expressed in the taste for the fashions of earlier times, and shamelessly exploited by nostalgia-merchants; memory has thus become a best-seller in a consumer society'.[4] Commenting on the three-part, seven-volume collective work *Les lieux de mémoire* which Pierre Nora edited over the course of the years 1984–92, Tony Judt remarks that 'to judge from the virtual disappearance of narrative history from the curriculum in many school systems, including the American, the time may soon come when, for many citizens, large parts of their common past will constitute something more akin to *lieux d'oubli*, realms of forgetting – or, rather, realms of ignorance, since there will have been little to forget'.[5] Richard Terdiman focusses the problem in a longer perspective when he writes that 'beginning in the early nineteenth century, we could say that disquiet about memory crystallized around the perception of two principal disorders: *too little memory*, and *too much*'.[6] Ulrich Beck focusses the question of forgetting in a future perspective; though the word forgetting is never mentioned in his discussion of humanly produced future risks, for example those issuing from nuclear or chemical contaminants and pollutants in foodstuffs, forgetting is a subtext to his discussion; for even as conjectures or prognoses, as hazards which may not be at present visible and in some cases may take effect only within the lifespans of the children of those now becoming preoccupied by risks, 'the centre of risk consciousness lies not in the present, but *in the future*', with the consequence that 'in the risk society, the past loses the power to determine the present. Its place is taken by the future, ... as the "cause" of current experience and action.'[7] Antoine Compagnon, finally, implies that we should think of our current spatial mobility as issuing in forgetting; shuttling back and forth between New York and Paris, as he has been doing for some years, he confesses to losing all sense of feeling at home in either language or culture, of having a strange sense of distance from whatever 'here' he is in, so that, closing up shop on one side of the ocean and opening up shop on the other side, 'You instantly forget all the numbers and names but those of your two or three closest friends. When you come back the curtain lifts and you remember it all again. Without this unnatural capacity to forget, you would never really be anywhere.'[8]

Yet, telling though they certainly are, most of these observations are intuitive suggestions. They whet the appetite and leave us longing for more. The subject of how modernity forgets has not so far been subject to systematic scrutiny. This it evidently merits.

To begin with the concept of modernity itself: by modernity I mean the objective transformation of the social fabric unleashed by the advent of the capitalist world market which tears down feudal and ancestral limitations on a global scale, and psychologically the enlargement of life chances through the gradual freeing from fixed status hierarchies. Chronologically, this covers the period from the mid nineteenth century accelerating to the present. Although this is a worldwide process, the examples I shall offer of forgetting are specific and much of the time located in the United States and Europe, on the assumption that these are the sources that produce the forgetting.

To say that modernity is characterised by a particular type of forgetfulness is to presuppose a conception of remembering. Remembering, therefore, needs to be delineated to make clear the meaning of forgetting. There are, of course, different kinds of memory; but there is one particular type to which I shall return repeatedly in a kind of circling insistence in what follows. This is place memory.

That memory is dependent on topography is an ancient insight. The so-called 'art of memory' was located within the great system of rhetoric that dominated classical culture, was reborn in the Middle Ages, flourished during the Renaissance, and only entered upon its demise during the period from the invention of printing to the turn of the eighteenth century.[9] Cicero gave a succinct statement of its operative principle. 'Persons desiring to train this faculty of memory', he writes, 'must select places and form mental images of the things they wish to remember and store those images in the places, so that the order of the places will preserve the order of the things.'[10] Accordingly, this 'art of memory' was described as a 'method of loci'. A locus is definable as a place easily grasped by the memory, such as a house, arch, corner, column, or intercolumnar space. The loci or places in question can be actually perceived or they can be simply imagined. The real or imagined place or set of places functions as a grid onto which the images of the items to be remembered are placed in a certain order; and the items are then remembered by mentally revisiting the grid of places and traversing them step by step. The premise of the whole system is that the order of the places will preserve the order of the things that have to be remembered.

Two features of the art of memory should be emphasised here. One is that it depends essentially upon a stable system of places. The other is that remembering relates implicitly to the human body and that acts of memory are envisaged as taking place on a human scale; some practitioners of the art speak of the rhetorician as walking around his memory-building as he seeks to imprint upon his mind the long sequences of thought which he wishes to remember.

These two features of the art of memory give us vital clues, I believe, for understanding the type of forgetting which is characteristic of modernity. A major source of forgetting, I want to argue, is associated with processes that separate social life from locality and from human dimensions: superhuman speed, megacities that are so enormous as to be unmemorable, consumerism disconnected from the labour process, the short lifespan of urban architecture, the disappearance of walkable cities. What is being forgotten in modernity is profound, the human-scale-ness of life, the experience of living and working in a world of social relationships that are known. There is some kind of deep transformation in what might be described as the meaning of life based on shared memories, and that meaning is eroded by a structural transformation in the life-spaces of modernity.

NOTES

1. F. Jameson, 'Postmodernism and consumer society', in H. Foster, ed., *Postmodern Culture* (London and Sydney, 1985), p. 125.

2. E. Hobsbawn, *Age of Extremes: The Twentieth Century* (London, 1994), p. 3.

3. A. Huyssen, *Twilight Memories: Marking Time in a Culture of Amnesia* (New York and London, 1995), p. 5.

4. J. Le Goff, *History and Memory* (New York, 1992), p. 162.

5. T. Judt, 'The past is another country: myth and memory in postwar Europe', in I. Deak, J. T. Gross and T. Judt, eds., *The Politics of Retribution in Europe: World War 2 and its Aftermath* (Princeton, 2000), pp. 293–324.

6. R. Terdiman, *Present Past: Modernity and the Memory Crisis* (Ithaca and London, 1993), p. 14.

7. U. Beck, *Risk Society* (London, 1992), p. 34.

8. A. Compagnon, *The 5 Paradoxes of Modernity* (New York, 1994), p. vii.

9. See F. A. Yates, *The Art of Memory* (Chicago, 1966); M. Carruthers, *The Book of Memory: A Study of Memory in Medieval Culture* (Cambridge, 1990); P. H. Hutton, *History as an Art of Memory* (Hanover and London, 1993).

10. Yates, *The Art of Memory*, p. 2, quoting Cicero, *De oratore*, II, lxxxvii, 351–4.

2　Two types of place memory

Many acts of remembering are site-specific, but they are not all site-specific in the same way. Consider, for instance, the following two cases.

My first example comes from the experience of contemporary Palestinians, for whom the primal event in their collective memory is the catastrophic uprooting of 1948, the dispossession and occupation brought about by the establishment of the state of Israel. Hundreds of their villages were destroyed, virtually all their homes and buildings demolished, and the sites reshaped by the new occupiers. In documents, in short stories, in paintings and in memory maps the fate of trees yields a condensed image for the catastrophe of uprootedness and the longing for rootedness. The emblematic status of trees is grounded in the actual fate of trees. The booklet *Olive Trees under Occupation* documents the experience of the village of Midya in 1986 when, after more than 3,300 olive trees were uprooted, black banners were raised at the entrance to the village and on individual homes, as when mourning the death of a person. In Ghassan Kanafani's short story 'Land of Sad Oranges' of 1987, the narrator, a young boy, on seeing his uncle's pain when he thinks of the orange trees 'abandoned to the Jews', recalls that a peasant back home once told him that the orange trees would shrivel and die if left in the care of strangers. In a painting by Amin Shtai of 1977 the combined figure of an olive tree and a man are represented, marked as Palestinian with traditional headgear; the arboreal trunk and the human torso merge into a single gestalt, with one tree leg and one human leg forming the lower part of the trunk. When Palestinians try to reconstruct memory maps of their destroyed villages, trees provide the leitmotif of their mnemonic quest; indeed, Palestinian pilgrims to these sites have little else but trees with which to do the work of memory and mourning.

My second example comes from the traumatic experience of agoraphobia reported by a number of European women in cities in the late nineteenth century. The term agoraphobia, together with the first coherent case studies of the illness, was first coined by Westphal in 1872. His patients, all men as it happens, reproduced with inexplicable personal anxieties the social taboos on movement in public places imposed on bourgeois women. In subsequent studies of agoraphobia, women constituted a large majority of the patients treated; they complained of an intense anxiety which rendered them incapable of moving around as everyone else did – unable to leave their house, to cross a deserted street or square, to enter a crowded concert hall. In fact they were experiencing as hysterical misery an everyday unhappiness of the nineteenth century. To the bourgeois mind of the time the street was a dangerous space; the social war, latent in the capitalist relations of production, was blatantly revealed on the street. When Engels described the condition of the working class in England in the 1840s he showed that the conditions of the working class and the conditions of their streets were the same. He described streets in Manchester, but also in London, Dublin and Glasgow, in Leeds, Bradford and Edinburgh. The streets were symptomatic. Since trade had become a man's job while the woman had her work within the domestic sphere, a man's presence on the street was legitimate, but women on the street were assumed to have gone there to work of necessity since their husbands could not provide for their family single-handedly. Hence men felt permitted to commit impertinences towards women who appeared on the street unaccompanied. We learn about the limitations imposed on the appearance of bourgeois women in the public sphere above all from manuals of etiquette. In her book on good manners, Mrs Van Zutphen van Dedem devotes a chapter to the 'act of avoiding and excluding'. A number of places were to be avoided: slums, local trains, streetcars, third-class pubs, cheap seats at movie theatres, crowds and celebrations in the streets.

Beyond this, the more refined person would be careful to avoid, as far as possible, the slightest contact with the bodies and garments of other people, because, even greater than the hygienic danger of contamination, was the ever present danger of contact with the spiritually inferior who might swarm into one's vicinity in densely populated city centres. The street was a threatening space.

By the last decade of the nineteenth century the limitations imposed on the appearance of women in public were beginning to disappear. Though there were ladies' compartments on trains and separate coffee houses for women, these segregations were gradually abandoned and women began to appear more freely in more places. And yet, precisely at a time when the social restrictions imposed on their movements in West European cities were decreasing, psychiatric journals began documenting case studies of agoraphobia suffered by women patients. The restrictions on the movement of bourgeois women prompted by a concern for their safety and status, which acquired added implications of respectability, chastity and dependency, now lived on in the form of fantasies about the street as a scene of potential violence and possible erotic encounters. Actions that had previously been socially prohibited, but were now permitted, remained unfeasible or problematic for at least some women, who became a prey to fantasies which, having withdrawn from the sphere of public discourse, found expression in agoraphobic anxieties as a problem to be treated by psychiatrists. At a time when the earlier restrictions on the movement of bourgeois women in public places were being relaxed, an agoraphobic relationship to public spaces continued to reproduce such restrictions in the form of hysterical compulsions while denying any grounds for their existence other than an inexplicable anxiety. This now inexplicable anxiety was the site of a collective memory. The memory that a particular locus was threatening took up residence not in etiquette manuals but in psychiatric symptoms.

For these two examples I am indebted to Carol Bardenstein and Abram de Swaan.[1] As it happens, both concern traumatic memories, but this is not the feature to which I wish to draw attention. They serve my present purposes by indicating two quite different ways in which the act of remembering may be related to or dependent upon a particular place. In order to register this difference I suggest that we distinguish between the *memorial* and the *locus*.

I

Taking this distinction as a cue, it becomes possible to survey a number of places according to whether they fall into one or the other of these two categories. As examples of the *memorial* we might consider the place-name and the pilgrimage. As examples of the *locus* we might consider the house and the street.

i

Memorial places can be as spare as place-names. For it is a simple but universal attribute of places that, like persons, they have individual names. Place-names can be more than markers and delimiters of place, more than tokens used to mark out and negotiate positions in social interaction. When they are semantically transparent, as they are for the Western Apaches, they are so powerfully evocative of incidents in well-known stories, they act so effectively as the mnemonics of a moral geography conjuring up exemplary behaviour, that the mere mention of a place-name encapsulates a well-known narrative.[2] More usually, place-names are semantically opaque: they cover the past of a place, half-hide a history. Often the history they hide will be about the capacity to exercise power over land and over others; the testimony remains when the power has gone. This is so of many English place-names, which track the itineraries of invasions and colonialism. The Scandinavian conquest of much of England from the late ninth century onwards resulted in old English villages being taken over and a great number of new villages founded, many hundreds of which bear pure Scandinavian names, most easily recognisable by the suffix *-by*. The names of Norwegians who settled in the north-western counties of England in the tenth century left traces

of their presence in the place-names of this region, as in the numerous *thwaites* of Cumberland and Westmorland. The post-Conquest
woodland clearances, most of them first recorded in the twelfth and
thirteenth centuries, are still indexed in scores of English place-names
from Yorkshire down to Devon, in Woodcotts, Woodmancotes and
Woodhalls.[3] Some place-names tacitly lament that there really is
nothing to memorialise, they tell a history of powerlessness in the
form of remoteness, of being virtually nowhere, as in the fields of
East Anglia named wistfully after far away places – China, Siberia,
Babylon, End of the World.[4] Some place-names are 'new' versions of
toponyms in their land of origin, as is New York, named at a time
when the English, in common with other European colonial settlers,
began to name remote places in America, Africa, Asia, Australia and
Oceania after settlements in the metropole.[5] Sometimes, then, place-
names are the site of two incompatible geographical imaginaries: as
in the Roper Valley in north Australia, where the Aborigine place-
names refer to ancestral action in a mythical time when the form
of the earth was supposed to be set forever, signifying the spiritual
force that is conceived to lie beneath the surface of the earth, and
having the continuing capacity to produce the present in the form
of the past, to enable new trees to grow, new people to be born, yet
with names which reunite the new with the old, collapsing all gen-
erational distinctions; whereas the English place-names in the Roper
Valley refer almost entirely to the late nineteenth and early twentieth
century, recording the actions of the early official 'explorers', whose
names form a scattergram of historical events registering changing
local use over time.[6] And again, terms like Middle East and Far East
are still anchored in our cognitive repertoire; even today they imply
a vista of power centred, literally and figuratively, upon a view from
the Greenwich Meridian.

At the moment when names are assigned to places, those who
do the naming are often particularly aware of the memories they
wish to impose. In France the great Revolution of 1789 signalled its
foundational claims by inscribing revolutionary toponyms on the

map of Paris. As early as 22 June 1790, the Constituent Assembly considered the question of appropriate names for the 48 sections of Paris, and the revolutionaries went on to debaptize 16 out of its 26 squares and 5 out of its 12 bridges. An honorific system distributed the names of Voltaire, Rousseau, Mirabeau, Buffon, Helvétius, Lafayette and Franklin across the Parisian street map in 1791–2. This was followed by a great surge of debaptisings in 1792–4 when names reminiscent of the monarchy and church were replaced by revolutionary names; Place Louis XV became Place de la Révolution, Pont Notre-Dame became Pont de la Raison. The ideal now was to represent the Revolution as the origin of History; the only memory that mattered was that of the objectives to be accomplished in the Future, the ideals, and therefore the toponyms, of the Rights of Man, Union, Law, the Sansculottes. Napoleon then brought the reign of toponymic abstractions to an end. He saw that if the present was to be glorified the past must be commemorated so that a necessary pedigree of national legitimacy could be put in place; so he picked out 'historical' names, long antedating the *Ancien Régime*, that is to say those taken from the period before Louis XIII. But the most visible aspect of his empire was the invasion of Parisian cartography by the names of his officers and battles: Rues d'Austerlitz, d'Iena, d'Ulm; and though Louis XVIII ordered the restoration of pre-revolutionary names to 49 Parisian streets, quays, squares and bridges, the 200 new streets which Napoleon had bequeathed to the city continued to glorify his name and achievements. To this day the symbolic geography of the capital cuts the Seine in two perpendicularly into the binary opposition of east/left and west/right. On the left bank is to be found the Panthéon, the civic temple of great men since 1791, Voltaire, Rousseau, Hugo, Jaurès; on the right bank is the statue of Napoleon in the Place Vendôme, and the Arc de Triomphe at l'Étoile. On 10 May 1981, François Mitterand celebrated electoral victory at the Place de la Bastille; on 30 May 1968, the supporters of Charles de Gaulle demonstrated on the Champs Élysées.[7]

In natural as in urban topography, in Papua New Guinea for example, toponyms are mnemonics, highly charged linguistic symbols.[8] Here it is impossible to talk about places without encompassing biographies; place-names summon up an immense range of associations, about history, about events, about persons, about social activities; and historical narratives are given precision when they are organised spatially, when temporal order is given shape as a sequence of localities associated with events. For Wamirans each stone, each tree, each dip in the ground has a name and a story, and identity is claimed and rights acquired through association with specific places in the landscape marked by stones. For Foi place-names are short-hands, encapsulating stories about historical or mythical events, and toponyms provide a mnemonic system for recalling the historical actions of persons which have made certain places singular and significant. For Kaluli, living in a terrain where acoustic information far exceeds that made available through vision, acute hearing is of paramount importance for locational orientation. The sensual primacy of water is transparent in their naming practices: natural forms linking together different watercourses or marking changes in land elevation – a conjunction where two waters come together, or a waterfall – mark out boundaries that coordinate landforms and waterforms in such a way as to demarcate boundaries, rights and fishing areas; and maps evoking memories of events and social relations are constructed in songs and laments whose emotional and memorial power depends on toponymic sequences.

ii

When we think of place-names we think of spare markings and of spatial fixity; but memorial places can also take the form of more elaborated codes and be attached to the more transient structures of spatial movement. Much ceremonial action, for instance, is performed by bodies moving in set ways within entire prescribed places: in kivas, plazas, longhouses, temples, churches. That particular form of bodily movement entailed in the crossing of a threshold is an important act in marriage, adoption, ordination and funeral ceremonies. We commonly speak of such ceremonies as rites of passage, and in doing so we are inclined to think of the action in question as a matter of diachronic development, as the temporal passage from one stage of life to another. But it is difficult for us to comprehend this *as* a temporal passage. We grasp this idea of temporal passage by means of our sense of place. When he came to analyse such rites of passage as a threefold process of separation, transition and incorporation, van Gennep described this tripartite process in terms of place.[9] It was 'territorial passage', he stressed, that provides the proper framework for understanding ritualised passage in the social sphere; again and again we find that the passage from one social position to another is identified with the entrance into a village or a house, or the movement from one room to another, or the crossing of streets and squares; and it is this identification built on territorial passage which explains why the passage from one group to another is so frequently expressed ritually by passage under a portal. The door is the boundary between the foreign and the domestic worlds in the case of an ordinary dwelling, and between the profane and the sacred worlds in the case of a temple. Repeatedly we find this movement from one place to another evoking the concept of the threshold as the specific zone in which a crucial transition is effected; to cross the threshold is to unite oneself with a new world. Not as *any* place, only as *this* particular, unsubstitutable place, can the threshold provide the unequivocal support for a rite of passage.

In the pilgrimage the threshold and the liminal state are particularly extensive. The pilgrimage is a long journey to a most sacred place, and it used to take many months, or even years. Even though large numbers of people still visit pilgrimage centres today, the process of pilgrimage is no longer integrated into the wider sociocultural processes of everyday life. But in medieval Europe and in Asia it was. To cite two examples only: there were in England during the medieval period at least seventy-four well-attended pilgrimage sites, and in Scotland, before the Protestant Reformation, thirty-two. When flourishing pilgrimage systems of this kind are integrated into the wider processes of everyday life, the optimal conditions for such integration were to be found in societies based mainly on agriculture, with a fairly advanced degree of craft labour, with feudal or patrimonial regimes, with a well-marked urban–rural division, but with only limited development of modern industry. Under such circumstances the pilgrimage journey marked one pole in a polar system of life. At one pole, daily life was lived in a rather sedentary fashion in village, town, or city; at the other pole, there was the rare phase of nomadism that was the pilgrimage journey.[10]

A pilgrimage journey can be made within a pilgrimage, a mnemonic place performed within a more expansive geographical imaginary. During his papacy, between 1585 and 1590, Sixtus V set out to change the image of Rome as a pilgrimage centre. His new Rome was built in five years. Ostensibly, his desire was to turn the whole of Rome into a single holy shrine. A new set of road connections were to link the seven main churches and shrines which had to be visited during the course of a day's pilgrimage. The whole of Rome was criss-crossed with a network of major streets and all existing buildings demolished if they stood in the way of the plan. A web of roads connected the church of Trinità del Monti and the great basilicas of Sta Maria Maggiore, San Giovanni di Laterano, Sta Croce in Gerusalemme and San Lorenzo fuori le Mura. Not all of the rebuilding of Rome derived from the initiative of Sixtus V. The three roads converging on the piazza already existed, and the two domed churches at their junction were not built until 1660. But it was Sixtus' idea to erect an obelisk at the spot where the sight-lines of the three roads met. This was one of a system of obelisks marking the intersections of the road system, the overt purpose of which was to make it easier for pilgrims to find their way from church to church: the columns and obelisks were signposts. These signs shepherded the throngs of pilgrims for whom Rome was the telos of a long journey. Long before the papacy of Sixtus V vast crowds of pilgrims had been arriving in Rome. In 1450 the crush of pilgrims crossing the Ponte Sant'Angelo on their way to St Peter's was so great that large numbers were pushed off the bridge and drowned. During the last decades of the sixteenth century the numbers of pilgrims arriving in Rome reached new heights: in 1575 Sta Trinità put up 174,467 pilgrims and in 1600 about 210,000 were looked after there. By then these pilgrimages had layered meanings. The core layer was the end of the pilgrimage journey to the main churches and shrines of Rome. Added to this was the wonderment of the new Rome of the late sixteenth century. In the course of only five years and four months Sixtus' initiative had so transformed the urban fabric of Rome that one priest returning there after Sixtus' death wrote that he could hardly recognise the city, that everything seemed to be new – edifices, streets, squares, fountains, aqueducts, obelisks. Subtending these two layers was a third, that of pre-Christian Rome. Christian pilgrims also visited the ruined wonders of classical Rome which were allotted a place in the *Mirabilia Urbis Romae*, the popular pilgrim's guide to Rome, first written in the mid twelfth century, and copied with additions and variations for several hundred years. To walk through Rome was to walk through an open-air museum. By the late sixteenth century Rome was a palimpsestic pilgrimage place. Many years later Henry James wrote of Rome as an infinite superposition of history.

The pilgrimage journey may be shaped either by spatial interdictions or by spatial injunctions. Among the modern Australian Aborigines the Walpiri employ the expression 'to go around' a place to express what we might speak of as making a detour. And the term for the Central Muslim pilgrimage, the hadj, probably derives from the old Semitic root *h-dj*, which means 'to go around'. Though both idioms refer to prescribed bodily movement within the spatial field of the pilgrim's journey, the expression 'to go around' had in the two instances entirely different significations: in the one case as an interdiction, in the other case as an injunction. Interdictions, as in the example of modern Australian Aborigine spatial taboos, might take the form of executing a detour around a place which must remain far enough away to avoid seeing it; if you can see what you are avoiding you are already too near. By performing a detour the actor carves out, as it were, a negative space, where they do not go, and part of this space may extend well beyond their own field of vision; by an act of exclusion, a specific kind of spatial form is produced, a space of deletions and delimitations.[11] A more frequent feature of the pilgrimage journey is the spatial injunction, which requires the approach to what may be described as the sacred centre of gravity; here the route becomes ever more sacralised as the pilgrim moves towards the central shrine.[12] At first, for instance in the journey to Jerusalem, the pilgrim covers many miles of mainly secular, everyday terrain in a subjective mood of penitence; but in the final stages of the journey almost every landmark, every step, is a condensed symbol, freighted with affect. The pilgrim's sense of the sacred is never private, but it becomes ever less private the nearer the journey approaches to the centre of its magnetic field. The closer the pilgrim approaches his telos, the more will objectified, collective representations encompass and suffuse virtually the whole environment. It is a matter of approaching, not the anxiety of influence, but the beneficence of influence.

The case of the pilgrimage shows how erroneous it would be to abstract the question of space from the question of bodily action. Whether it is a matter of spatial interdictions or of spatial injunctions, what is happening is that persons produce a symbolic nexus out of the interaction between bodily actions and terrestrial places. Even the term pilgrimage itself can be misleading in this connection. The Sanskrit word for pilgrimage, for example, is *yatra*, a 'proceeding' or 'going', and in fact it is usually *tirtha-yatra*, a 'going to fords', meaning that pilgrimage places are sited on river crossings. And the Pali for 'going forth' is *pabbajja*, related to Sanskrit *pravrajya*, which means 'going forth', in other words leaving the life of the sedentary householder and taking to the life of homelessness as a wandering ascetic. These linguistic usages express what happens in a set of actions within a spatial field which more appropriately catches the sense of what is involved than does the reification implied in the abstract substantive 'pilgrimage'.[13] Speaking of social space generally, Henri Lefebvre writes of 'the basic duality' of space as a 'basis of action' and as a 'field of action'.[14] By a basis of action he means 'places whence energies derive and whither energies are directed'. By a field of action he means not the determinate region but the mobile spatial field of the actor: a field centred in the situated body with its immediate tactile reach, and extending into vocal scope, acoustic range and visual horizon. The body is a spatial field, and the pilgrim is, at every stage, located: where locatedness refers mainly to mobile actors rather than to things. If pilgrimage teaches us that we should not abstract the problem of space from the problem of bodily action, it does so by showing that spatial boundaries are not always fixed, relatively enduring forms marked off on the ground. And from the elaborated code of the pilgrimage journey we should draw the inference for the restricted code of place-naming: place markers can never be abstracted from the actions of spatially and temporally situated actors.

2

We can now shift our attention from the memorial as a memory place to the locus as a site of cultural memory.

i

The locus may encompass quite varying degrees of magnitude. Consider for instance the house. The sensation of being surrounded – in a room, a house, a valley, the enclosure of a horizon – is always with us. In the house the architect constructs an interior world with a minimum set of coordinates; with an inside/outside boundary, and cardinal points coordinating directions of existence, normally organised on a front/back axis. The working of a house as a set of coordinates, a memory device, depends on a degree of immobility. Even mobile homes are made to lose their look of mobility; a porch, a patio, a garden may help to bind the home to its environment, and trees also help to immobilise it.[15] The home becomes an aide-mémoire: of the ongoing necessities of everyday life by the spacing of provisions in the cupboards, where the most precious objects, those used on the grandest occasions, are placed on the highest shelves, while everyday provisions, which are cheaper to replace, are nearer to hand; of family rankings which are inscribed in interior space, the ordering of seating round the table corresponding to other orderings, to privileges and to birth; of the interweaving of individual life histories, with time devoted to the communal meal being used to coordinate arrangements, to diffuse information, and to weigh up and share evaluations of outside events and people.[16]

The house is not only, therefore, a building in which a group of people live. It provides more than a shelter and spatial disposition of activities, a material order constructed out of walls and boundaries. Over and beyond this it is a medium of representation, and, as such, can be read effectively as a mnemonic system. Many anthropologists agree on this point. The house has been compared to a book in which is inscribed a vision of the structure of society and the cosmos;[17] it has been compared to a social text, one of the best modes available in a preliterate society for embodying ideas, so that, in the absence of literature, the house illustrates not only particular principles of classification but the value of classification as such;[18] it has been seen as providing its inhabitants with a model for the structure of the universe because it can represent relationships irrespective of scale and the nature of the material parts out of which it is built;[19] houses have been compared to 'spatial texts', cultural representations in the form of metaphors for various kinds of social units and categories, such that actors are able to constitute meanings and different power relations through their everyday spatial practices.[20] People are able to transpose the system of the universe onto the concrete systems which they are able to shape by their practical actions, so that the Para-Pirana of Colombia, for example, build longhouses with a linear male–female axis running between the two doors and activities are organised around a concentric pattern in which the periphery represents private family life and the centre represents public, commercial life.[21] Again, the Fijian house is a map of Fiji hierarchy and etiquette; 'the side of the house toward the sea was called the noble side and with it went the east end or, if the house were perpendicular to the seashore, the east side was the noble one, and with it went the sea end'.[22]

If the house provides a mnemonic structure, that is not solely by virtue of its being a static medium of representation. There is the further dynamic circumstance that the life history of the house is interwoven with the life history of the body.[23] Both have in common a quality of taken-for-grantedness; just as we tend to take our bodies for granted until they fail us through accident or illness or ageing, so too we take houses for granted until exceptional circumstances, a house-moving or a family row or a fire or a war or penury, forcibly remind us of the house's central significance in our lives. There is another moment when these two life histories are graphically expressed: the projection of the self, which is a bodily self, onto the house, is clearly glimpsed in western children's drawings of houses which characteristically contain two windows and a door, features we might translate as two eyes and a mouth. The house's furnishings also remind us of the shared history of the house and the body. In the interior of houses artefacts are collected which give access to previous experience. In a study of contemporary Chicago, Rochberg-Halton finds that the objects actually valued in the house are not the 'pecuniary trophies' which functioned as 'reliable indices of one's socio-economic class, age, gender', but the artefacts embodying ties to loved ones and kin, and memories of significant life events; it is photographs and particular objects like a piano, clock or chair that generate a sense of the self that lies outside the sensory over-load of a society of consumption.[24] Nor are such objects likely to be randomly dispersed; it is above all at the centre point of houses that memories of the world outside the house are domesticated, retained and re-experienced. In the North American country house the hearth is customarily surrounded by memorabilia, just as in the Mexican country house the fountain in a courtyard frequently provides a centrepiece surrounded by memorabilia. The proximity of family treasures to the centre point of houses provides them with qualities yielding senses of touch and permanence. Nor should we think of the hearth simply as the symbolic centre; it has a further layer of meaning as the locus of transformations. Houses are not just static structures; they are continually transforming what passes through them, for it is at the hearth that the different elements that enter the house, kin and affine, meat and vegetables, are mixed and blended, so that the hearth is materially and figuratively the site where the history of these transformations takes place. There is a further parallelism. The Zafimaniry house solidifies and is extended together with the people who inhabit it, since house building is begun at the same time that a couple embarks on marriage and only completed when their first child is born; and the Makassarese compare house building to childbirth, a process completed only with the birth of three children. In this way architectural processes – building, maintenance, modification, extension – often coincide with important events in the lives of those who occupy houses, so that there are congruencies and echoes, of which the inhabitants cannot but be aware, between the life history of the house and the life history of the bodies inhabiting it.[25]

Some houses are particularly large and elaborate places, as are the meeting houses constructed by the Maori of New Zealand's North Island between about 1850 and 1930 to which Roger Neich has devoted a detailed study augmented by photographic documentation. Such meeting houses were a development of chiefly houses, large structures erected in the early nineteenth century and in the pre-European period, the aim of their construction being to diminish the self-esteem of members of rival communities and to exalt the ancestors of the house-building community over everybody else's ancestors by objectifying those ancestors in the magnificence and meaning of the houses.

Such houses are loci of memory. The house belongs not just to the present and not just to the temporal period of its construction, but to an extended period of time reaching back into the past while also drawing that past into the present. For Maori to enter a house is to move not only into the body of the house but to enter the belly of the ancestor and to be overwhelmed by this encompassing ancestral presence. Overhead there are the ribs of the ancestor, represented in the form of magnificently decorated rafters which converge towards the ancestral backbone, the ridge-pole, which objectifies the genealogical continuity of the chiefly line, which notionally proceeds by primogeniture.

Is not such a ceremonial home so far elaborated as a memory place that it no longer qualifies as a locus and belongs instead to the category of the memorial? The fact that this is not so has been demonstrated by Alfred Gell in a brilliant analysis. He shows that the Maori meeting house is, as a very large and complex artefact, an index of agency, an agency which is collective, ancestral and essentially political in tone. Since the 'agency of the ancestor', of which the house is an index, is future-oriented, it follows that the ancestor's body/house is, as he writes, 'not a corpse or a memorial to the departed'. Certainly the house explicitly conceptualises the body of the eponymous ancestor of the community; but this ancestor is, as Gell says, 'not so much "memorialised" in the houses which bore his name, as reinstated in this form'. Pushed to the very limit of complexity, the Maori meeting house is still a locus of memory.

ii

Or one might consider, as an example of the locus, the city street. Because it is difficult to control, the street is a possible zone of massive contestation and can turn into a special kind of political space. During the July Revolution of 1830 the streets of Paris were studded with 4,000 barricades;[26] in pre-revolutionary Russia the Nevsky Prospekt developed as a kind of free zone in which social and political forces could unfold spontaneously;[27] in East-Central Europe the demonstrations of 1989 took place especially in the streets. Even when it is not a space of open confrontation, the peripatetic possibilities of the street can harbour threatening encounters and disturbing memories.

In the mid nineteenth century many of the lumpenproletariat eked out a living as itinerant streetsellers with no fixed premises; streetsellers of food and drink numbered in London between 3,000 and 5,000 in 1851; and these formed only part of a motley group which included also vagabonds, discharged jailbirds, swindlers, pickpockets, ragpickers, tinkers and beggars – what Marx called the 'whole, indefinite, disintegrated mass thrown hither and thither', what Mayhew called the 'nomadic' or 'wandering' tribes.[28] Memory has much to do with the generic nature of particular experiences; and the nomadic topography of the nineteenth-century city street provoked extended commentary from contemporaries because it clouded the former demarcations which had made it possible to assign experiences to certain insulated categories, to say that one type of experience was tragic, another comic, one idyllic, another satiric. Now the literal closeness of one thing to another on the street precipitated an ambiguity in the genre of experience, an ambiguity exemplified preeminently in the writings of Dickens where the generic differences between comic, tragic, idyllic and satire are broken down. Still other types of contestation, of course, were more deeply repressed on the nineteenth-century street. The theorists of modernity – Baudelaire, Benjamin and Simmel, for example – were often particularly attentive to the experience of men in the public sphere of the street; by omission, if by that alone, they tacitly acknowledged the confinement of women to the private sphere. It might have been possible for some to feel at home in the privatised public space of the street, to survey the crowd, to stroll, stop and stare: as did Baudelaire, for whom the signs of street shops were as enthralling a wall ornament as an oil painting is to the bourgeois in his salon; or Dickens, who, when on Lake Geneva, nostalgically remembered Genoa where there were available to him two miles of streets by whose light he had been able to roam about at night. A man who did this became a flâneur; a woman who did it became a streetwalker. In the figure of Gervaise, Zola in *L'assommoir* imagines a working-class woman's perception of the boulevards; confronted by their grandeur, she feels cheap and overwhelmed, unable to occupy the space with ease, unable to make it part of her everyday memories, unable to make herself part of others' memories of the street.[29]

The inhabitants of city streets have memories of feeling cheapened and overwhelmed too when their streets are invaded by an army of occupation, as happened, for example, to Parisians between 1940 and 1944. At that time Robert Doisneau, Roger Parry and Roger Schall took a few striking photographs of occupied Paris, images of German soldiers on some of the most magnificent streets of Paris and of road signs piled high with Gothic script, signs of an oppression which remains in these images entirely unforgettable.

Aside from their aspect as a particular kind of political space, the best streets are those that are remembered. When you think about a city, whether your own or some other, you might quite probably think of some particular street, a street which has left a strong impression on you. It might be memorable because it brings order to a city or district, letting you know where you are by forming a boundary, as does the Ringstrasse in Vienna. It might be memorable because it acts as a spine, a central structural element to the surrounding area, with a strong beginning and ending, like a spatial narrative, as with the Via dei Giubbonari in Rome and Strøget in Copenhagen. It might be memorable because it gives focus to a city: as does Nevsky Prospekt in St Petersburg, or as do the three streets that lead from the Piazza del Popolo, with the Via del Corso in the middle, in Rome. Or again, there may be not a single street but an assemblage of streets of a particular type that is memorable: as with the French Quarter in New Orleans, or the system of canals in Amsterdam, or the assembly of arcaded streets, known locally as the 'streets with porches', in Bologna. It is above all the quality of providing a gestalt, of giving order and focus, that makes a street, or an assembly of streets, memorable.[30]

But to think of streets in this way is to envision them as if seen from the viewpoint of a static observer, as a vista scanned from a single point of vantage or as a shape discerned on a map. What this leaves out of account is the fact that it is not only a specific gestalt but a particular pace of assimilation that makes a street, and what is experienced there, memorable. Every fine street invites walking. There must be a route, safe from vehicles, that allows people to walk at varying speeds, including a leisurely pace, with neither a sense of being too crowded nor a sense of being too alone. One might think of Las Ramblas in Barcelona, a wide, tree-lined promenade, where pedestrians are assigned the preferred section of the right of way, in the centre, so that they set the tone and pace for the whole; or one might think of the Boulevard Saint-Michel in Paris, where it is difficult to walk fast in daylight and where books on tables and clothes on racks in front of stores attract the attention and slow the pace. To modify the pace, you are likely to find, somewhere along the line of a fine street, a break: a small plaza or a park or an open space. Especially on narrow or long streets they provide stopping places, points of reference. Even benches – they are plentiful on the Boulevard Saint-Michel, Las Ramblas, Strøget – help people to stay on a street, help to make community.

We should never underestimate the importance of street intersections. They act as sorting devices, precipitating encounters, some serependitous, some mildly embarrassing. The life of a city street is formed over time out of many such local contacts. You might get advice from a grocer, or you might stop at a bar for a beer, or you might run into someone you have not seen for some time and exchange a little pertinent information. In themselves these may all be trivial events, but the sum total of events of this kind is not trivial. The sum total of local public contacts, most of them fortuitous, none of them implying private commitments, builds a web of public trust. A spatial metaphor, that of the web, is not chosen at random in speaking of the net result of many little local occurrences; for spatial arrangements are here the causal agent. The crossing and re-crossing of people's routes depends on the spacing of street intersections. Jane Jacobs drew attention to the fact that, when street intersections were placed far apart, the mixing of people's paths which made up a sense of neighbourhood could not occur.[31] With long blocks people are kept too far apart to permit them to form reasonably intricate pools of city cross-use. Long blocks automatically sort people into paths that meet too infrequently, so that different uses which, geographically, might seem to be very near each other, when scrutinised on a map, are effectively blocked off from one another. Consider for instance the difference between Venice and Irvine, California.[32] The intersecting walkways and canals along the Grand Canal in Venice occur approximately every 23 metres of its length; whereas in Irvine you are not likely to find more than one public intersection for every 201 metres along a major street in the business district. The former conduces to community; in the latter you will feel very little sense of community. The frequency of street intersections in a street layout crucially affects the quality of urban life and the way in which that urban life is remembered by its participants. A street network becomes what one might call a memorable social text partly because of the way in which the street intersections are spaced in the web of the whole pattern. An urban street network is likely to be 'thick' in meanings the more richly it is endowed with street intersections, the more closely they are tied together. To devalue street intersections is to devalue civic memory.

Nothing, above all, is less plastic than the urban street layout. The housing system, as distinct from individual houses, is a massive permanence in a city; over time individual houses within a district will tend to change, but a residential district in the city may persist as such for centuries. Legal ties and property rights impose an invisible set of obstacles to change. Simply to widen a street requires destroying the houses that line it, at least along one side. Even when bombings have eliminated the urban buildings above ground, planners have had to repeat the plan. More than any component element, the urban plan is most resistant to change. One can study the persistence of a city's basic layout, its street plan, as one might study the persistence of a legal structure or that of a genealogical network. This concept of morphological persistence is spelt out in Rossi's observation that the Paris of today is like a composite photograph, one that might be obtained by reproducing the Paris of Louis XIV, Louis XV, Napoleon I and Baron Haussmann in a single image;[33] it is the guiding thread in Conzen's study of the morphology of the English city in the industrial age;[34] it informs Lavedan's history of urbanism;[35] it is fundamental to Poëte's monumental four-volume work on the life of the city of Paris from its birth to the twentieth century.[36] Poëte argues that, for all that the plan becomes differentiated in its attributes, in substance it is not displaced; cities tend to remain on their axes of development, maintaining the position of their original layout. In the broad avenues and boulevards, the public buildings, the parks and squares, the networks of sewers, Haussmann left a permanent impression on Paris. His street system of 1870 served the city well for nearly a century, only becoming clogged with the great influx of cars after the Second World War. Despite the supersession of horses by cars, the replacement of gas lights by electric lights, the additions of the Eiffel Tower and the Sacré-Coeur, Haussmann's Paris of 1870 would have been familiar to anyone who knew Paris in the 1950s.[37]

3

i

Viewed as a carrier of cultural memory, what is it about the memorial that distinguishes it from the locus? A significant part of the answer to this question consists in its different relationship to the process of cultural forgetting.

Many memorials are, admittedly, powerful memory places. Yet their effect is more ambiguous than this statement might imply. For the desire to memorialise is precipitated by a fear, a threat, of cultural amnesia.

It was when the age of mechanical reproduction caused objects to become obsolete at an ever accumulating speed that many Europeans devoted their energy to a cult of monuments without earlier parallel and founded public museums on an unprecedented scale.

One European country after another set up new legislation to ensure the preservation of ancient monuments,[38] while museums salvaged, collected and preserved what fell prey to the creative destruction of modernity.[39] In much the same way, when a nation feels itself to be no longer a place where history on a grand, a truly memorable, scale is being made, it turns inward to cultivate its memorials. After the devastation of Europe in 1918, after the deceptive victory of 1945 which marked the end of European hegemony, after the projection onto the world stage came to an end for Britain in 1956 and for France in 1962: then the self-doubt which accompanies the transition from a great power to, at the very most, a middle-range power, led to the politics of nostalgia in Britain and to the attempt at national self-definition of which Nora's project *Lieux de mémoire* is itself a memorial.[40]

As Piranesi makes clear in the preface to the four volumes of his *Antichità Romane* of 1756, his great plan of once more re-presenting the majesty of classical Roman space was conceived when he saw before his eyes its dispersal into a tumble of ruins;[41] it was when he first saw the remains of the ancient buildings of Rome lying in cultivated fields or gardens and wasting away under the ravages of time, or being destroyed by greedy owners who sold them as materials for modern buildings, that he determined to preserve them forever by means of engraving. Or yet again: sometimes what had once formed an impressive or forbidding spatial landmark becomes a memorial in the very moment of its dispersal; as when, in the immediate aftermath of the fall of the Berlin Wall, thousands gathered to acquire a fragment of a marker about to disappear; this emblem of the Cold War became a memorial when its fragments came into the possession of those who wanted their tangibility to provide a spur to future recollection of what was being made absent through decomposition.[42] This intimate link between memorialisation and the moment of felt transience surfaces again when the urge to build memorials to the Holocaust tacitly acknowledges the approaching final disappearance of those who are the only ones who can truly remember it, those who survived it; for it is these alone who can remember the smell of burning human flesh; and, as the Spanish writer Jorge Semprun writes, 'a day is coming when no one will actually remember this smell; it will be nothing more than a phrase, a literary reference, an idea of an odour'.[43]

The relationship between memorials and forgetting is reciprocal: the threat of forgetting begets memorials and the construction of memorials begets forgetting. If giving monumental shape to what we remember is to discard the obligation to remember, that is because memorials permit only some things to be remembered and, by exclusion, cause others to be forgotten. Memorials conceal the past as much as they cause us to remember it. This is evidently so with war memorials. They conceal the way people lived: where soldiers are directly represented in war memorials, their image is designed specifically to deny acts of violence and aggression. They conceal the way they died: the blood, the bits of body flying through the air, the stinking corpses lying unburied for months, all are omitted. They conceal the accidents of war: the need to make past actions seem consolingly necessary impels people to make sense of much that was without sense. And they conceal the way people survive. The Great War had undone so many: the International Labour Organization estimated in 1923 that about ten million soldiers from the German, Austrian, British and French armies peopled the streets of their nations. Care of the war wounded went unrewarded, often unnoticed, in millions of households who rarely received the material assistance they needed. The war dead were annually commemorated; the maimed and mutilated were forgotten as far as possible.[44] The war-wounded and war widows were routinely neglected because they provided the wrong kind of memory. But we are endlessly devious in expressing to ourselves the intolerable in a tolerable form. The gigantic gymnastic performances so fashionable in Germany and Central Europe during the 1920s and 1930s, regimented displays of fit, young, healthy, athletic bodies, was, literally, a *massive denial* of the fact that at the same time ten million mutilated war survivors haunted the streets of Europe, dismembered men many of whom were subject to chronic depression, succumbed to alcoholism, often went begging in the street simply to survive, and frequently ended their days in suicide. To notice them, still more to reflect upon their circumstances, was too disquieting. They themselves had no option but to confront their condition every day in the mirror. For others, the sight of them was not unpalatable, it was an indigestible fact. The annual incantation at war memorials, ritually intoned, – 'lest we forget' – did not apply to them.

ii

What is it, by contrast, that makes the locus, in its far more *inexplicit* reference to memory, such an effective carrier of cultural memory?

Part of the answer applies particularly to a historically particular type of culture, to the world before the age of mechanical reproduction. A *handmade* world, in which all things were made one by one, was a slow world. Only when we have thought ourselves imaginatively into such a handmade world can we comprehend the slow process in which, before the nineteenth century, the natural landscape and the urban landscape came into being. In sizeable European cities the construction of the city walls and the cathedral were the main events in the city's history for generations; just as a house is part of the biography of a family, so a great civic building project was part of the collective biography of the inhabitants of a city. The third city wall of Cologne, for instance, begun in 1180, was completed only in 1210.[45] Between the first siege of Vienna in 1529 and the last in 1683 the fortification of the walls of Vienna were continually being strengthened.[46] The sixth Florentine wall, built as a demonstration of political power, with a length of 8,500 metres, and a breadth of nearly 40 metres, with its 73 towers and its 15 fortified gates, took some fifty years to complete, between 1284 and 1333.[47] Almost every cathedral city spent fifty years or more building its cathedral; these vast construction projects were for decades a focal point of activity for hundreds of masons, stonecutters and sculptors. Even today the

Milanese call their cathedral 'la fabbrica del dôm', and understand by this expression the size and difficulty of the church's construction, the idea of a *process* of building which goes on over a long time. In a handmade world the term 'building' would apply as much to the memory of the *continuing transitive activity* of construction as to that of the eventual *product*.

But the effectiveness of the locus as a carrier of cultural memory applies also to all different kinds of historical settings.

Partly this is because of the *encoding* power of place. We need to distinguish here between intentional coding, a subject obviously susceptible to semiotic analysis, and the encoding of a sedimented tradition. In the latter case, we can look at the encoding, but those who built what we are looking at, although they built in an encoded way, were following habitual practices, as was the case in the building of houses in many English villages. Or again, there was in the nineteenth century in the United States a zoning of business districts. You went to the textile area and walked around there if what you wanted to find were textiles, but this zoning was a form of spatial disposition which had slowly grown up over time; it was not like Milton Keynes, it was not planned.

Encoding buildings in the strong sense of the term is markedly different. Then we can say, quite unequivocally,[48] that people build in a certain way because they think in a certain way, and they think in a particular way because they build in a particular way. Produced spaces and cultural rules interconnect because both indicate who permissibly communicates with whom, how, when, where and under what conditions. If we occasionally do a 'double-take' on seeing someone we have seen before but cannot quite 'place', that is usually because the present setting in which we happen to come across them is not the place where we normally encounter them; our initial difficulties in recognition arise because they are, as far as we are at that particular moment concerned, temporarily 'out of place'. At the time we encounter them, they happen to be outside the topographically coded space to which we customarily assign them. At one scale topographic codes have to do with our modes of inhabitation; there are common rooms, dining rooms, parlours, studies. At another scale certain architectural configurations unmistakably indicate building types; there are churches, railway stations, hospitals, restaurants. Sometimes linguistic terms refer to both space and to its use; lawcourts and choirs are both places and institutions. And in general abstract linguistic oppositions – public/private, sacred/secular, lawful/criminal – become comprehensible to us in material spaces. Topography is a rhetoric, a set of well-tried discursive formulae.

But there is a world of difference between topography as a rhetoric that is *known about*, and topography as a rhetoric that is *known*. The concept that a person has of an urban artefact will always differ from the concept of someone who 'lives' that same urban artefact. For there is a type of experience recognisable only to those who have walked through a particular building or street or district. Only they have lived it. To 'live' an artefact is to appropriate it, to make it one's own. This does not mean, of course, that it becomes one's own possession, one's property, but that one makes it one's own by making it one with, ingredient in, one's continuing life. As I know my way around the limbs of my body, as a pianist knows her way around her piano, as I know my way around my own house, so I know my way around the paths, landmarks and districts of my city. For me no longer to know my way around the limbs of my own body, perhaps through amputation, or for a pianist no longer to know her way around her piano, perhaps because of failing eyesight, is tearfully distressing, an aching catastrophe: as it would be to no longer know my way around my own house, or no longer to know my way round the paths and landmarks and districts of my city. That would be a defamiliarisation that would shake my very being. For familiar places are appropriated by my lived body that has, as Merleau-Ponty said, a knowledge bred of familiarity that does not give us a position in objective space, but a sense of emplacement through their incorporation into the corporeal life of my habitual movements.

Topography as a rhetoric that is, in this sense, known is at once cultural and multisensory. It is cultural, in the sense that relationships to places are not lived exclusively or even mainly in contemplative moments of social isolation, but most often in the company of other people and in the process of doing something with them. It is multisensory, because, to borrow a fine formulation of Steven Feld's, as places are sensed, senses are placed, and as places make sense, senses make place.[49] A sense of place depends upon a complex interplay of visual, auditory and olfactory memories. Because sound is central to Kaluli experience in the tropical rainforest, for example, there are local conditions of acoustic sensation and knowledge embodied in the culturally particular sense of place resounding in Bosavi; and just as the memories precipitated by the life-space of a Gothic cathedral are unthinkable without the acoustic enrichment which this particular architectural form makes possible,[50] so an intentional acoustic deprivation was fundamental to the intricately planned prisons of the nineteenth century, involving as they did a minute and extensive investigation of the construction of cell walls so as to make them as totally soundproof as possible.[51] Sadism produced sound deprivation.

The memory of particular types of emplacement feeds particular dispositions. We might be tempted to speak of dense and varied as well as anonymous and fleeting encounters as being the type of interactions which mark the atmosphere of life in big cities; but we ought to avoid the elision of place hidden within the phrase 'atmosphere of life' and refer it instead, quite specifically, to certain spatial settings, for example that of railway stations, where there is generated the horizon of expectations in which encounters of precisely this kind – encounters that are dense and varied as well as anonymous and fleeting – regularly occur. Again, we might speak of modernist architecture as a 'container' architecture of office blocks, department stores and congress centres; but we ought to reflect rather on the way in which the absence of relationship with an immediate environment which is so marked a feature of such functional container buildings habituated people to an obliviousness regarding the wider ecology which surrounds our built topography, effacing awareness and respect for the very existence of such an ecology. Or again, if an advertisement were to be strictly functional, without any ornamental surplus, it would no longer fulfil its function as advertisement; and the history of advertisement over the last hundred years has executed a trajectory from the more functional to the more ornamental, from the explicit and spare to the oblique and ornate; as the telos of the advertisement unfolds, the life-spaces which are ever more saturated by such artefacts produce a generalised disposition to surplus, a ubiquitous expectation of ornamental visual surfeit which extends to other artefacts and becomes naturalised as a form of life. It is in such ways that cultural memories engendered by particular types of emplacement reproduce particular cultural dispositions.

There is, in other words, a certain matter-of-factness, a *taken for grantedness*, which distinguishes our experience of a locus from our experience of a memorial. A memorial has something in common with a work of art, in the sense that we assume that a work of art, a painting or piece of sculpture, is a more or less demanding message, explicitly addressed to us, something that asks of us a focussed interest, a degree of concentration, even absorption. A glance, a transient registering of its mere existence by our peripheral vision, would never do justice to a well-executed painting, and a war memorial of which we were entirely oblivious would have failed of its purpose. Many war memorials, as a matter of fact, do precisely that. As Musil once said, nothing is more invisible than a memorial. But we experience a locus *inattentively*, in a state of distraction. If we are aware of thinking of it at all, we think of it not so much as a set of objects which are available for us to look at or listen to, rather as something which is inconspicuously familiar to us. It is there for us to live in, to move about in, even while we in a sense ignore it. We just accept it as a fact of life, a regular aspect of how things are.

This is the power of the locus. That is why the locus is more important than the memorial – whose construction is so often motivated by the conscious wish to commemorate or the unavowed fear of forgetting – as a carrier of place memory.

NOTES

1. C. B. Bardenstein, 'Trees, forests, and the shaping of Palestinian and Israeli collective memory', in M. Bal, J. Crewe and L. Spitzer, eds., *Acts of Memory* (Hanover and London, 1999), pp. 148–68; A. de Swaan, 'The politics of agoraphobia', in *The Management of Normality* (London and New York, 1990), pp. 139–67.

2. K. Basso, ' "Speaking with names": language and landscape among the Western Apache', *Cultural Anthropology*, 3: 2 (1988), pp. 99–130; and 'Wisdom sits in places: notes on a Western Apache landscape', in S. Feld and K. H. Basso, eds., *Senses of Place* (Santa Fe, 1996), pp. 53–90.

3. W. G. Hoskins, *The Making of the English Landscape* (London, 1955), pp. 70, 72, 88.

4. C. O. Frake, 'Pleasant places, past times, and sheltered identity in rural East Anglia', in S. Feld and K. H. Basso, eds., *Senses of Place* (Santa Fe, 1996), pp. 229–57.

5. B. Anderson, 'Memory and forgetting', in *Imagined Communities* (London, 1991), pp. 187–206.

6. H. Morphy, 'Colonialism, history and the construction of place: the politics of landscape in northern Australia', in B. Bender, ed., *Landscape: Politics and Perspectives* (Oxford, 1993), pp. 205–43.

7. D. Milo, 'Street names', in P. Nora, ed., *Realms of Memory* (New York, 1996), vol. II, pp. 363–89.

8. S. Feld, 'Waterfalls of song: an acoustemology of place resounding in Bosavi, Papua New Guinea', in S. Feld and K. H. Basso, eds., *Senses of Place* (Santa Fe, 1996), pp. 91–136; M. Kahn, 'Your place and mine: sharing emotional landscapes in Wamira, Papua New Guinea', in S. Feld and K. H. Basso, eds., *Senses of Place* (Santa Fe, 1996), pp. 167–96.

9. A. van Gennep, *The Rites of Passage* (Eng. tr. Chicago, 1960).

10. V. Turner, *Process, Performance, and Pilgrimage* (New Delhi, 1979).

11. N. D. Munn, 'Excluded spaces: the figure in the Australian Aboriginal landscape', *Critical Inquiry*, 22 (Spring 1996), pp. 446–65.

12. Turner, *Process, Performance, and Pilgrimage*.

13. Munn, 'Excluded spaces' .

14. H. Lefebvre, *The Production of Space* (Eng. tr. Oxford, 1991).

15. K. Harries, *The Ethical Function of Architecture* (Cambridge, Mass., 1997), pp. 99, 144–8, 172, 248–50.

16. M. Douglas, 'The idea of a house: a kind of space', *Social Research*, 58: 1 (Spring 1991), pp. 287–307.

17. J. Carsten and S. Hugh-Jones, eds., *About the House – Lévi-Strauss and Beyond* (Cambridge, 1995); P. Bourdieu, *Outline of a Theory of Practice* (Eng. tr. Cambridge, 1977), p. 89.

18. C. Cunningham, 'Order in the Atoni house', *Bijdragen tot de Taal-, Land- en Volkenkunde*, 120 (1964), pp. 34–68.

19. P. Wilson, *The Domestication of the Human Species* (New Haven, 1989), p. 58.

20. H. Moore, *Space, Text and Gender* (Cambridge, 1986).

21. C. Hugh-Jones, *From the Milk River: Spatial and Temporal Processes in Northwest Amazonia* (Cambridge, 1979), p. 246.

22. M. Sahlins, *Culture and Practical Reason* (Chicago, 1976), p. 33.

23. Carsten and Hugh-Jones, eds., *About the House*, Introduction.

24. E. Rochberg-Halton, *Meaning and Modernity: Social Theory in the Pragmatic Attitude* (Chicago, 1986), p. 173.

25. M. Bloch, 'The resurrection of the house amongst the Zafimaniry of Madagascar', in J. Carsten and S. Hugh-Jones, eds., *About the House* (Cambridge 1995), pp. 69–83.

26. W. Benjamin, *Charles Baudelaire: A Lyric Poet in the Era of High Capitalism* (Eng. tr. London and New York, 1973), p. 15.

27. M. Berman, *All that Is Solid Melts into Air* (New York, 1982), pp. 195–205, 263, 276.

28. K. Marx, in *Marx-Engels Selected Works* (Eng. tr. London, 1951), vol. i, p. 267; H. Mayhew, *London Labour and the London Poor*, 4 vols. (London, 1851–2), vol. i, p. 2. See also P. Stallybrass and A. White, 'The city: the sewer, the gaze and the contaminating touch', in *The Politics and Poetics of Transgression* (London, 1986), pp. 125–48.

29. On the impossibility of the flâneur as a woman see J. Wolff, *Feminine Sentences: Essays on Women and Culture* (Berkeley and Los Angeles, 1990).

30. A. B. Jacobs, *Great Streets* (Cambridge, Mass., 1993).

31. J. Jacobs, *The Death and Life of Great American Cities* (London, 1962), pp. 191–9; see also A. B. Jacobs, *Great Streets*, pp. 37, 48, 53–5, 143–4, 161, 195, 202, 302.

32. A. B. Jacobs, *Great Streets*, pp. 221–2, 259–61, 302.

33. A. Rossi, *Architecture and the City* (Eng. tr. Cambridge, Mass., 1982), p. 142.

34. M. Conzen, 'Zur Morphologie der englischen Staat im Industriezeitalter', in H. Jäger, ed., *Probleme des Städtewesens im industriellen Zeitalter* (Cologne, 1978), pp. 1–48.

35. P. Lavedan, *Histoire de l'urbanisme*, 3 vols. (Paris, 1926–52).

36. M. Poète, *Une vie de cité. Paris de sa naissance à nos jours*, 4 vols. (Paris, 1924–31).

37. D. H. Pinkney, *Napoleon III and the Rebuilding of Paris* (Princeton, 1958).

38. M. C. Boyer, *The City of Collective Memory* (Cambridge, Mass., 1996).

39. A. Huyssen, 'Escape from amnesia: the museum as mass medium', in *Twilight Memories: Marking Time in a Culture of Amnesia* (New York, 1995), pp. 13–35.

40. P. Nora, ed., *Realms of Memory*, 3 vols. (Eng. tr. New York, 1996–8).

41. T. Cooper, 'Forgetting Rome and the voice of Piranesi's "Speaking Ruins"', in A. Forty and S. Küchler, eds., *The Art of Forgetting* (Oxford and New York, 1999), pp. 107–25.

42. S. Küchler, 'The place of memory', in A. Forty and S. Küchler, eds., *The Art of Forgetting* (Oxford and New York, 1999), pp. 53–72.

43. J. Semprun, *Literature and Life* (London, 1998).

44. J. Winter, *Sites of Memory, Sites of Mourning* (Cambridge, 1995), p. 46.

45. W. Braunfels, *Urban Design in Western Europe: Regime and Architecture 900–1900* (Eng. tr. Chicago and London, 1988), p. 25.

46. Ibid., p. 295.

47. Ibid., p. 50.

48. U. Eco, 'Functionalism and sign: the semiotics of architecture', in M. Gottdiener and A. Lagopoulos, eds., *The City and the Sign* (New York, 1986), pp. 56–85.

49. Feld, 'Waterfalls of song', p. 91.

50. 'The greatest church of early Christendom was the Basilica of St Peter, forerunner of the present Renaissance edifice in Rome. It was an enormous, five-aisled building with stone columns separating the aisles ... the acoustical conditions of such a church must by their very nature lead to a definite kind of music. When the priest wished to address the congregation he could not use his ordinary speaking voice.

If it were powerful enough to be heard throughout the church, each
syllable would reverberate for so long that an overlapping of whole
words would occur and the sermon would become a confused and
meaningless jumble. It therefore became necessary to employ a more
rhythmic manner of speaking, to recite or intone. In large churches
with a marked reverberation there is frequently what is termed a
"sympathetic note" – that is to say "a region of pitch in which tone is
apparently reinforced". If the reciting note of the priest was close to
the "sympathetic note" of the church ... the sonorous Latin vowels
would be carried full-toned to the entire congregation. A Latin prayer or
one of the psalms from the Old Testament could be intoned in a slow
and solemn rhythm, carefully adjusted to the time of reverberation.
The priest began on the reciting note and then let his voice fall away
in a cadence, going up and down so that the main syllables were
distinctly heard and then died away while the others followed them
as modulations. In this way the confusion caused by overlapping
was eliminated. The text became a song which lived in the church
and in a soul-stirring manner turned the great edifice into a musical
experience. Such, for instance, are the Gregorian chants which were
especially composed for the old basilica of St Peter in Rome ... Thus,
in the old churches the walls were in fact powerful instruments which
the ancients learned to play upon.' S. E. Rasmussen, *Experiencing
Architecture* (Cambridge, Mass., 1959), pp. 226–30.

51. 'Expectations about reformation [of prisoners] required as near total
silence as possible in each cell to induce necessary reflection and
introspection. Before work began on the Model Prison, therefore,
the first task was to construct a totally soundproof cell. Not only
did these ideas require a different prison plan; they also demanded
research into new construction techniques as well as building services.
Experiments were begun inside the perimeter wall at Millbank Prison.
The inspectors first tried cell walls 31 inches thick consisting of two
13-inch jagged walls separated by a 5-inch space. As these were not
totally soundproof, two thicknesses of sailcloth were hung in the 5-inch
space, but this was difficult to accomplish; moreover, the sailcloth
rotted in the damp air. The inspectors then tried building two 9-inch
brick walls, with two spaces of 3¾-inch divided by a 4½-inch brick
wall in the middle. This prevented intelligible communication but

resulted in considerable reverberation when the side walls were struck, so the 3¾-inch gaps were filled with sand. Yet, while diminishing the vibration, this experiment made the cells less soundproof. The same experiments were repeated with Bath stone instead of brick; ultimately, the inspectors settled for 18-inch walls, double doors, arched ceilings and concrete floors, to prevent the penetration of any comprehensible noise.' H. Tomlinson, 'Design and reform: the "separate system" in the nineteenth-century English prison', in A. D. King, ed., *Buildings and Society* (London, 1980), pp. 99–100.

3   Temporalities of forgetting

Many modern material practices are implicated in the process of cultural forgetting. To observe these in operation we need to distinguish between different categories of temporality, where by temporality I mean institutionalised and organised time schedules which crucially structure a person's experience of time. The different temporalities I want to distinguish are: the time of the labour process; the time of consumption; the time of career structures; and the time of information and media production. In each case, I want to suggest that the specific type of modern temporality entails an abbreviation of history and a corresponding form of cultural forgetting. Two further corollaries should be noticed. First, each particular temporality reinforces the others to precipitate a reciprocally interlocking cascade of temporalities; it is their combined effect which generates a systematic form of cultural forgetting. Secondly, none of the temporalities can be understood without comprehending the spatial dimensions which are ingredient and intrinsic to them.

I

The modern world is the product of a gigantic process of labour, and the first thing to be forgotten is the labour process itself. At one level, of course, to say this might seem puzzling or even perverse; working time is made explicit under capitalism as never before; making the most of available time becomes the supreme principle for human activities and technological artefacts. For human beings: because time-discipline means that they are perpetually pressed for time. For technological artefacts: because machines can 'survive' economically only when they are adaptable to shortage of time, with the predictable end result that in information-intensive technologies they attain velocities far exceeding human perception. Under capitalist social formations, then, certain forms of social relations are quite transparent in the undisguised adversarial positions of capitalist and worker over the explicit control over working time. What, by contrast, becomes opaque is that form of time essential to the transformative process of labour.[1] The one notion essential to any form of social production, the sole transhistorical condition of social life, according to Marx, is human labour; labour is that condition of human existence which mediates what he calls the 'metabolism' between man and nature. In the *Grundrisse* he indicates the essential implication of this conception for the temporality of labour: the fact that there is a purposiveness animating human labour which gives it directionality. 'Labour', he writes, 'is the living, form-giving fire; it is the transformation of things, their temporality, as their formation by living time.'[2]

These words are cryptic and condensed, and they need spelling out further. We might do so in the following way. Some human creative capacities appear to leave behind no palpable traces or to leave traces which no sooner appear than they rapidly disappear – witness housework, cooking – whereas other human creative capacities leave a visible precipitate in the form of created objects. In these cases the human maker projects into the made object the maker's power of creating. A coat, for instance, is a made object invested with the human capacity to create, and it exists to complete the task of recreating us by making us warm. What the human maker projects into the made object may vary from object to object, but what he or she will always project into it is the power of creating. Every day we encounter a world of such manufactured objects. These objects will commonly contain no personal signatures affixed to them, so that we are unable to know or infer who the maker is; but as Elaine Scarry has put it, the objects will contain what might be called a general human signature;[3] though the name of the person who manufactured the coat, or part of the coat, will not be found in the coat, there may be a label in the seam or in the interior of the collar indicating the company to which that person belonged; and even if we cannot discover such a label, we can infer, from the seams and collar, that the coat did have a human maker or makers. The convention according to which painters affix their *personal* signature to their completed canvasses derives part of its meaning as a signifying practice from the implicit and tacitly understood contrast between this 'personal' act of creation and the 'impersonal' act of creation pertaining to the world of infinitely replicable manufactured objects.

Every day we encounter such manufactured objects, but since many of these objects have no seams or cutting marks that record their origins in human creativity we quite naturally remain ignorant of their origins. As we move each day through the sphere of manufactured objects – dishes, cars, newspapers, streetlights, city parks – we do not at each moment consciously perceive that these objects are humanly made whereas we do precisely that when we move through an art gallery. We misperceive the objects, to the extent that we treat them as if they had a merely 'objective' existence. Once an object has escaped from the hands of its producers it takes on what Marx calls a 'phantom-like objectivity', and leads its own life. Appearing at first glance to be at once trivial and self-sufficient, a commodity becomes an abstraction. But once we think about it we begin to see it as a bewildering abstraction. And when an infinity of objects are packed into the expanding space of a giant city our misperception is likely to grow exponentially. A city is unthinkable without an infinity of hinterland linkages. The market of which it forms a nodal point in space fosters exchange relationships of immense range and complexity, while at the same time obscuring those relationships from us in the very process of creating them. If we live in a city we consume goods and purchase services in a marketplace with linkages to people and places who remain invisible to us, unknown to us, and perhaps unimagined by us.

While certain features of capitalist social relations are transparent, such as the prolonged struggle over the control of *working time*, other features of those relations are opaque, specifically *the temporality of the labour process as a whole.* This opacity of the labour process has of course been referred to customarily as reification. Reification is a form of fetishism: fetishism being the transformation of human capacities into the apparent attributes of 'things': technological inventions, laws, rhetorical conventions, which now appear 'natural' and therefore 'binding', their meanings as the precipitates of human creative capacities being no longer properly understood. Reification, the illusory objectivity of a mechanism which appears to operate by its own independent laws, much like the laws of nature, arises on the basis of a specific social formation – that is, the structuring of the work process by the exploitation built into the particular institution of surplus value, that is, profit. The fundamental transformative practice of human labour, what might be called the *diachronic process* of labour time, is misperceived as the *illusory synchronicity* of exchange-value. The labour process is obscured. In his great essay on reification in *History and Class Consciousness*, Lukács argued that the capitalist process of production was *constituted by the loss of its memory* of the very process through which it is produced.[4] As an organised structure of misrecognition, it blocked access to recollection of the past processes which erected it and maintained it in being. In trying to penetrate this veil of opacity, Lukács, building on the work of Marx, sought to decipher the 'imprint on the whole of consciousness of what is usually called the "commodity form"', his basic argument being that the precise details of the structured process of producing commodities gets *forgotten*. In other words, the genesis of the commodity form, the human agency that creates manufactured artefacts in this particular social formation, falls prey to a cultural amnesia. Since the labour process is rendered opaque, certain crucial memories about how this type of society is produced are made unconscious, the production of commodities being, at the most significant level, made unavailable to consciousness.

If Marx, and following him Lukács, Benjamin, Horkheimer and Adorno, insists repeatedly on the bewildering abstraction of the commodity form, there is frequently an undeniably abstract vein in the language in which they themselves seek to decipher this phenomenon. That this is evidence more of the bristling difficulties and relative intractability of the problem they are confronting, rather than simply linguistic self-indulgence on their part, is suggested if we now partially shift linguistic register to consider briefly one symptom which they themselves do not mention but which their diagnosis prompts us to alight upon as a particularly revealing symptom of the condition they are diagnosing. I mean the literary genre of detective fiction. It is surely no accident that classic detective fiction reached its peak between about 1890 and about 1935, since it can be read, as a genre, as symptomatic of that condition of increasing opacity which characterises capitalist social formations. The central theme of the detective story, as Franco Moretti has shown, is the search for clues in a social field that appears at first sight to be indecipherable.[5] As Holmes says repeatedly to Watson: 'You see but you do not observe.' If Watson could observe properly, he would be capable not just of knowing that money is always the motive of crime, but of being able to read particular clues which would lead him finally to the perpetrator of a particular crime; and he would be able to do so, because he would track down successfully something irreducibly personal that betrays that individual: traces that only that particular person could have left behind. 'Singularity is almost invariably a clue. The more featureless and commonplace a crime is, the more difficult it is to bring it home', as Holmes tells Watson in *The Boscombe Valley Mystery*. He specifies the point further when, in *A Case of Identity*, he remarks that 'A typewriter has really quite as much individuality as a man's handwriting.' The object of detective fiction is always to decipher these clues in order to return to the beginning. The implied reader of the detective story is incited to follow the plot and in so doing to arrive at the motive in the desire for profit; but always – and this is crucial – to seek it in the sphere of circulation, so that the implied reader is forever coming across thefts, frauds and false pretences. Money is always the motive in detective fiction; yet the genre remains silent about *production*, that is to say, about the labour process: that unequal exchange between labour-power and wages which is the true source of social wealth.[6] The detective, a successful seeker after the particular origin of crime, a virtuoso of memory when it comes to connecting clues in pursuit of that quest, operates within a literary genre in which the *real origin* of money in the labour process is forever forgotten. This is why detective fiction, as a genre, is symptomatic of that condition of opacity which characterises capitalist social formations.

Rarely, however, is the problem of deciphering the opacity of the labour process more vividly illustrated than in the instance of place. One particular place, and the history of that place, makes this opacity perfectly tangible: the development of Chicago in the late nineteenth century, as William Cronon has demonstrated in his brilliant history of Chicago.[7] At that time Chicago became the greatest railway centre in the world because it was the link that tied together east and west into a single system. Eastern railways south of the Great Lakes would reach their *western* terminals in Chicago, and the various western railways fanning out from the city would reach their *eastern* terminals in Chicago. As a Chicago railway analyst once said, western roads were built *from* and eastern ones *to* Chicago. Chicago was the nodal point where the westward flow of merchandise complemented the stream of natural resources flowing in the opposite direction. Country people sent grain, lumber and livestock to Chicago, receiving in exchange an endless variety of manufactured goods which they bought with the produce of their land and labour, and which were assembled by Chicago wholesalers for distribution to rural and small-town customers throughout the city's hinterland to the west. The city streets of Chicago were the places where the products of different ecosystems came together and exchanged places.

Opaque? What could be more transparent? Indeed, all the relevant information about the merchandise in which you might be interested was spelt out in the mail-order catalogue. There you could read in the advertisements about the links between the metropolis and the hinterland, about the flow of debt and credit, about the structure of the distribution system as a whole. Yet take a closer look at the way in which the mail-order catalogue is constructed. On its pages each product stands alone, simply one more item among tens of thousands which a customer might wish to consider. Having identified the product, there was no need for the customer to wonder where it came from, or how it had been created, or by whom, or with what implications for the place in which it had been made. The customer could see perfectly clearly that the product he or she was interested in came from Ward or Sears. The answer to all these other hypothetical questions stopped at Chicago. One could buy merchandise after consulting a Montgomery Ward catalogue without troubling to reflect on a web of economic and ecological linkages that stretched out in all directions. The natural roots from which it had sprung or been extracted and the human history of the labour process that had created it faded from view as it passed along the long chain of wholesale–retail relationships. The relationship in which the flow of merchandise was enmeshed was obscured from view.

Or, in other words, they were forgotten. As natural ecosystems became more intimately linked to the urban marketplace of Chicago, they came to appear ever more remote from the busy place that was Chicago. Chicago both fostered an ever closer connection between city and country, and concealed its debt to the natural system that made it possible. Chicago concealed the very linkages it was creating. The field was separated from the grain, the forest from the lumber, the rangeland from the meat. The more concentrated the city's markets became and the more its hinterland expanded, the easier it became to forget the ultimate origins of the things bought and sold there. The easier it became to obscure the connections between Chicago's trade and its earthly roots, the more casually one could forget that the city drew its life from the natural world around it.

One might feel discomfort at the proposition that commodification, or the fetishisation of commodities, which disguises the labour comprising manufactured and sold objects, is a matter of 'forgetting'. Other ideas that have been used here to describe that process are 'false consciousness', or 'misrecognition', and indeed the term 'fetishisation' would be a competing idea. Or one might equally well speak of simple 'ignorance', or of a process of 'mystification', and indeed Braudel shows the existence of processes of relative ignorance created by the expanding commerce of the late Middle Ages. But we should retain the concept of forgetting, I suggest, for the following reason. The notion of forgetting here is extended from something an individual might do in an everyday sort of way to something societies, or indeed civilisations, might do. So really the notion of forgetting on a societal scale is to suggest two things: first, that the collective representations held knowledge about the matter in general for all competent participants; and second, that the knowledge was progressively lost.

As Raymond Williams and John Barrell among others have emphasised, obscured connections envelop the countryside as a generic space just as they configure the city as a generic space. What we speak of when we refer to the 'countryside' consists of relatively uninhabited land. It is not those who actually live and work in these landed areas, customarily designated 'the country', but those who live and work outside those areas – estate owners, improvers, industrialists, artists – who customarily talk the language of landscape. It is they who invented the concept of landscape. Once scrutinised, their conventional usage of the idea of landscape discloses an otherwise concealed ambiguity in the concept of landscape, which installs and maintains in existence a disjunction between 'insiders' and 'outsiders'. The idea of landscape implies the denial – perhaps it is its unacknowledged intention to deny – of the fact of the human labour process. By highlighting the land's visual, painterly features, the idea of landscape is not simply a privileged but a restrictive way of seeing which promotes the 'outsider's' point of view, while sustaining in existence a radical split between 'outsiders' and 'insiders' on the land: between those who relate 'directly' to the land, and those who relate 'indirectly' to the land as a form of exchange-value. For the insiders, the local people, the land is a place where they make their living, mainly through farming, with tractors and noisy machines. For them, 'nature' is the physical basis for their agricultural labour, and the long distances and cost entailed in maintaining necessary connections with suppliers and markets is experienced as remoteness. For the outsiders, often professional people in the media and arts, the land is a place suffused with romantic associations with 'nature'; it offers a site of withdrawal from their professional worlds where they can earn the incomes which enable them to retreat to sites of seclusion. If these outsiders are able to 'read' the land as a place of romantic seclusion – and this particular mystification of landscape is especially marked, of course, in the history of English reactions to landscape, as the counter-statements of Williams and Barrell indicate – they can only do so by seeing it and misperceiving it simultaneously: farmers and farming, the daily and yearly grind of the labour process in that area, are entirely erased from the outsider's perspective. Once again, the labour process is forgotten.[8]

From the city to the country we can extend the idea of place further still to embrace the land of a nation-state; and in doing so we find the process of forgetting recurring once more. In a lecture entitled 'What is a Nation?', delivered at the Sorbonne in 1882, Ernst Renan singled out as perhaps the crucial trait of a nation the anonymity of its membership; a nation is a large collection of people whose members identify with the collectivity without being acquainted with the other members and where the remaining links with groups predating the emergence of the nation tend to become rarer and more tenuous. France, he claimed, had taught mankind this principle of nationality, the idea that a nation exists through itself and not by virtue of a dynasty. More recently, Eugen Weber has demonstrated exhaustively that France was less culturally unified in the 1880s than Renan had then assumed it to be.[9] Among an array of evidence, he cites a pioneer statistical essay of 1836, which concludes with the observation that there were two nations in France, divided by the now familiar imaginary line running from Saint-Malo to Geneva: north of the line, peasants were fewer but taller, better fed, better educated, better housed, and relatively easy to recruit for military service; south of the line, peasants were shorter, worse fed, worse housed, and slow to accept conscription. This was the geographical division, between the poor, backward countryside of rural France, and the other areas of France, rural or not, that were to some degree permeated by the values of modernity, which had to be effaced if France was to form a cohesive national unity. Eugen Weber has shown that, between about 1880 and about 1910, such fundamental changes occurred in France that these early years of the Third Republic were as important as any other, and more important than most, in effecting the transition from traditional France to modern France. He singles out three changes in particular. French peasants became habituated to military service. French education taught hitherto uneducated millions of people the language and values, patriotism included, of the dominant culture. And roads and railways brought hitherto remote regions into easy contact with modern markets. In consequence, the regions of France were vastly more alike in 1910 than they had been in 1836. In demonstrating this, Eugen Weber, while modifying Ernst Renan's claim about the historical timing of the process, provides overwhelming evidence to endorse Renan's basic insight. A shared amnesia, a collective forgetfulness, Renan asserted, was at least as essential for what we now consider to be a nation as is the invocation of common memories: 'Forgetting', he declared, 'I would even go so far as to say historical error, is a crucial factor in the creation of a nation.'[10] Eugen Weber has put us in a position where we are able to state what is entailed in Renan's argument more precisely. Of those causes he highlights, we should never underestimate the importance of new transport networks, in road and rail, which linked hitherto inaccessible regions to the markets of the modern world. When peasants were turned into French citizens, they had to forget partially that they were peasants in order to learn that they were French citizens; and this process of forgetting was, to a significant degree, accomplished through the many repercussions of the labour process.

In other words, when we speak of a place such as Chicago, or the countryside, or France, we are always in danger of forgetting that these are places created in long processes of labour. Their identity is always, and always has been, in process of formation. The identity of place is always embedded in the histories which people tell of them, and, most fundamentally, in the way in which those histories were originally constituted in processes of labour. Whenever we talk about places, what is at issue, whether we acknowledge it or not, are competing versions of the histories in the process of which the present of those places came into being. Whenever we speak about the identity of a place, therefore, we run the danger of imputing to that place a false 'essence', by abstracting it from the history of the place itself.[11]

This abstraction from the history of places is a habitual reaction all the more deeply latent because we frequently and as a matter of course think about places in spatial terms, as when we indicate them as points or areas on a map, and say that they are located there, or that they extend over that area. Our perception of place is filtered through this spatial mapping as grains of coffee are filtered away before drinking a cup of coffee. Yet in automatically thinking of places as represented on maps, we are yet again entangled in a process of forgetting, because in the historical process the labour of producing places is followed by the labour of producing *spatial mappings of places*. This secondary labour, once more, entails a process of effacement and forgetting. We can only understand how this comes about by noticing the distinction, to which de Certeau has drawn attention, between an *itinerary* and a *map*.[12] An itinerary represents a particular route or routes, with starting points and destinations; it indicates how to get from one to the other. A map represents a region in a way which is entirely indifferent as regards starting points and destinations. When Florentines discovered in the Ptolemaic system a cartographic device for collecting geographical knowledge according to the same principle of geometrical harmony which they expected of their art, they became able to represent the most dispersed places as precisely fixed in relation to one another, by means of unchanging mathematical coordinates, such that these proportionate distances became apparent. It was in the course of the period characterised by the birth of modern scientific discourse, between the fifteenth and seventeenth centuries, that the map, representing not a *route* to be traversed but a *state* of geographical knowledge, eliminated from its frame of reference the activities of travel that preceded it and of which it is the result. These previous itineraries were effaced, though they were not effaced all at once; as representations, early modern maps were frequently hybrid constructions, containing upon their surface two incompatible orders of representation.[13] The proliferation of narrative figures – ships, animals – still indicated the travels which were the precondition of the map's later construction; the sailing ship painted on the sea indicated the maritime expedition that made it possible subsequently to represent the coastlines, and it remained a sign, pointing to the memory of travel and exploration. But gradually these *signs of memory* became effaced; the map eliminated the pictorial figures which represented the laborious practices necessary to produce it. In the new cartographic space that was abstract, homogeneous and universal, map-making was characterised precisely by the erasure – the forgetting – of itineraries.

The inclination to forget the labour process entailed in the production of places is pervasive. Such forgetting is most vividly displayed in certain favourite idioms, as when people speak of 'the power of place' or of the 'genius loci'. Fetishism reappears here because to talk in this way is to imply that places – cities, neighbourhoods, localities, regions – possess causal powers independent of their creators. Yet place is never a fixed spatial entity but always a social process in transformation; as David Harvey has stressed, we ought to ask why, by what means, and in what sense, do subjects, acting together in labour processes, invest places, financially and emotionally, with that degree of permanence which causes them to become the locus of institutionalised power and culturally specific perception.

The process of forgetting has usually been spoken about, by Marx and others after him, in technical terms, as when they write of fetishism or reification. When they resort to figurative language to explain their cultural diagnosis, the reservoir of metaphors they draw on derives most commonly from idioms of speech referring to visual perception. They speak of opacity, occlusion, obscurity, lack of transparency, difficulties in deciphering. Almost certainly, their privileging of visual imagery derives ultimately from the thought that sight occupies a special and distinctive position among all other sense perceptions, a conviction of the nobility of sight already announced by the classical Greek philosophers, and subsequently reiterated by many generations of western philosophers, who thought of their activity as being in some crucial sense like that of a person who holds a mirror up to the nature of things, and of vigorously polishing that mirror, in the strenuous effort to get as precise a perception of the true nature of things as might conceivably be accomplished.[14] It was from this *idée maîtresse* that there flowed the inclination to suppose that any form of miscognition or distorted cognition could most helpfully be comprehended, figuratively speaking, as a deficiency of visual perception, where such a sense defect was tacitly understood to be a synecdoche for misperception as such. Nonetheless, Marx and others after him also quite frequently speak of forgetting, and when they use the verb to forget as a synonym for what they write about in technical vocabulary as fetishism or reification, and in metaphorical language as defective vision, they are perfectly aware of this alternative linguistic usage and of what they mean by it. So they write that the commodity seems enigmatic because people forget how it was produced; or they say that people forget that the origin of profit is in the surplus value extracted from human labour; or they insist upon the fact that the human agency that creates manufactured objects gets forgotten; or they draw attention to the fact that the more concentrated and extensive city markets become the easier it is to forget the ultimate origin of the things that are bought and sold there. It is quite legitimate, therefore, to redescribe the process most frequently diagnosed as reification or the fetishism of commodities as a process of forgetting. Indeed, Adorno made the point succinctly: 'All reification', he writes, 'is a forgetting.'[15]

2

Culturally induced forgetting is reinforced by the temporality of consumption. To buy objects for consumption is to participate in commodity exchange rather than to engage in gift exchange. Marx's analyses of commodity exchange, which he sees as producing a reified perception of things, and so effectively a form of cultural forgetting, was deficient to the extent that he believed that, historically, the practice of exchange developed from being transparent to being opaque. This overlooks the fact that both commodity exchange and gift exchange are encoded. There is no transparency about gift exchange, whether it is viewed as a sequential chain or as a strategic set of acts by particular agents; in either case gift exchange needs to be decoded as a system of obligations. The effects of the two forms of encoding are quite different, however, with respect to their consequences for remembering and forgetting. The mode of encoding operative in gift exchange precipitates a form of cultural remembering; the mode of encoding operative in commodity exchange generates a form of cultural forgetting.

Gift exchange potentiates memory because, as Mauss first perceived, it rests upon a triple obligation: the obligation to give, the obligation to receive, and the obligation to reciprocate. In certain cultures, to refuse to give, or to fail to invite, is tantamount to declaring war. A chief has an obligation to give a Potlatch for his son-in-law, for his daughter and for his dead. Each Kwakiutl and Haïdu noble therefore has precisely the same idea of 'face' as has the Chinese man of letters or official; it was said of one of the great mythical chiefs who gave no Potlatch that he had a 'rotten face' and the obligation to invite is particularly clear when it is extended to those outside the family, the clan, or the phratry; it is essential to invite anyone who can come, or who wishes to come, or who actually turns up, at the Potlatch festival. Then, secondly, there is the obligation to receive. In certain cultures, a clan or a household is obliged to receive presents, and to enter into trading and to contract alliances. Just as one has no right to refuse a gift, so one has no right to refuse to attend the Potlatch, for to do so would show that one is afraid of having to reciprocate. If a gift of food is accepted, the recipient knows that the gift comes with a burden attached. A challenge has been accepted, because the invitee is confident of the capacity to reciprocate. Since the unreciprocated gift makes the person who has accepted it inferior, particularly when the gift has been accepted without any thought of reciprocation on the part of the recipient, each gift is part of an obligatory system of reciprocity involving the honour of giver and recipient. When he discovered this mechanism for inserting individual interests into a cultural system without engaging in market exchanges, Mauss found in the cycle of gift exchange a rejoinder to Adam Smith's commodified invisible hand; by providing persons with incentives to collaborate in structural exchanges, the gift cycle complements the market cycle to the extent that it remains in operation when the latter is absent.

The triple obligation to give, to receive and to reciprocate forms a memory chain of obligations, a chain which is further reinforced by the manner in which this set of obligations is discharged. The mode of discharging obligations may be viewed from the perspective of the system of exchange, or from the standpoint of the agent acting within the system; by either route you will end up by recognising the ways in which gift exchange reinforces memory.

If you view the exchange of gifts as a system – as when important Trobriand islanders exchange Kula objects, armshells and necklaces which conventionally have to be exchanged against each other, with their dependants or with those whom they wish to put in that position – you will stress, as Malinowski did, the circulating of Kula exchanges. Malinowski found that some fourteen groups of islands were involved in Kula, forming a circle: generally, necklaces travelled clockwise, armshells anti-clockwise, with each type of object completing a circle within a period of time ranging between two and ten years, depending mainly upon the number of exchanges between islands involved in the circulation of Kula.

If, on the other hand, you view Kula from the perspective of the agent who takes advantage of the system in order to attain worldly renown, you will emphasise the way in which such persons plot and scheme to manipulate the path along which a Kula valuable travels, forming a chain of reciprocal obligations between one man and another. These pathways are generally marked by previous exchanges: as when a man gives because he has received, or when he gives because he wants to oblige some person to give him what he wants, or when he diverts a particularly valuable gift from one possible recipient to another because he has decided that he will gain by doing so since he perceives the partner on the original pathway to be of lesser importance than the partner on the alternative track. But in other cases a person may be so bold as to initiate a new pathway, in which case he will always be aware that everybody else in his home group will be watching this and talking about it, and that, should he have a rival for worldly esteem, which he most probably will, that rival will be observing events too and will be utterly delighted if everything goes awry. All these exchanges will be *remembered*.

So whether you view what is going on in Kula exchange from the viewpoint of the system or from that of the agent, you will always be alerted to the power of gift exchange as a generator of cultural memory. This mnemonic power is lacking in a system of commodity exchange. Further, the effacement of remembering which that entails becomes still more noticeable if one focusses on a feature of commodity exchange which becomes increasingly perceptible in the course of a very long-term historical trend. For in the system of commodity exchange the temporality of consumption is increasingly characterised by the *aestheticisation of commodities*.

Culturally induced forgetting is reinforced by the temporality of consumption, which renders ever more inaccessible to immediate perception the process of reification intrinsic to commodity exchange by focussing attention ever more insistently on immediate perception. The temporality of consumption is marked above all by the *aestheticisation of commodities*.

Industrial capitalism did not, of course, usher in all at once the aestheticisation of commodities within whose medium we now swim as fish in water. In *Society of the Spectacle* of 1967, Guy Debord writes that 'the entire life of societies in which modern conditions of production reign announces itself as an immense accumulation of spectacles';[16] but these modern conditions were not even a gleam in the magpie eye of an entrepreneur at the opening of the nineteenth century. In Adam Smith's *Wealth of Nations* of 1776, the commodity is conceived as anything but an aesthetic phenomenon; it is viewed simply as a form of exchange subject to the laws of supply and demand, the structure of distribution being taken for granted. The exchange of commodities is thought of as a channel for the passage of money, and is described as something similar to the operation of natural laws, as when Smith likens it to the circulation of the blood, or on other occasions to the force of gravity, when he writes that the market price of every particular commodity is continually gravitating towards the natural price. Once commodities have been manufactured, Smith considers them 'work done'; even the examples of commodities which he cites – for example, pins – makes it clear that he does not see them as encircled by a nimbus of the aesthetic.

The slow shift of emphasis from the use-value to the exchange-value of commodities, on the part of their producers and purveyors, was tracked by a significant conceptual adjustment, on the part of the diagnosticians. Marx had been inclined to posit a dichotomous relationship between production and representation; the forces and relations of production he saw as the locus of the real, representation – for instance, in the form of theological or legal arguments, or classical political economy – as a discursive veil concealing those relations. He expended much analytical resourcefulness in trying to establish the logical separability of the two terms. But by the late nineteenth century a number of German economists, impressed by the phenomenon of the nineteenth-century exhibitions, were prompted to propose an intermediary term between the concepts of production and representation; by what they called the 'Ausstellungswert' of commodities they intended to denote the *productive capacity of representation itself*; by which they meant to underline the fact that commodities gain added value by virtue of their mode of appearance, quite apart from their use-value.[17] Subsequent developments in the aestheticisation of commodities – captured most succinctly in a Situationist graffito of May 1968, 'Merchandise is the opium of the people' – validated the necessity of this conceptual move, by making it ever clearer that advertising is the mythicisation of commodities, their transformation into a fetish that openly parades its fetishism, spotlighting its more arcane features rather than hiding them. Advertising becomes not so much the exhibition of 'a' commodity as rather 'commodity fetishism' *tout court*; or, in other words, Marx's fetishism of commodities raised to a higher power of mystification. This more recent historical development is most evidently exemplified in the ludic practice of particularly *oblique* advertising, in which the more arcane semiotic implications of proffered commodities are knowingly and teasingly flaunted, so as to challenge and incite the viewer into a collusion of bewitchment, the spectator being spurred to track and hold on to the thread that still connects 'representation' and 'reality', while being nudged all the time in effect into questioning whether either of the two terms, the 'real' and the 'representation', might still validly apply to two cognitively distinguishable fields.

It was in the expositions of the nineteenth century that a gradual shift of emphasis took place from the *use*-value to the *exchange*-value of commodities. When the celebration at the Crystal Palace in 1851 set a limited number of manufactured objects within the confined space of the exhibition, while at the same time conjuring up within that spatial confinement the anticipation of unprecedented surplus, an aestheticisation of the commodity form was already being envisioned. But within the enframed space of the exhibition, what has now become habitual to us as the society of the spectacle was still in an embryonic condition. This is made evident, above all, by the catalogue to the exhibition; here attention is focussed squarely on the *use-value* of objects.[18] The catalogue contains references to specimens from an enormous range of raw materials on which industry operated throughout the world; all the different types of wood used in furniture, for instance, were itemised, with their commercial names, their Latin names, their native habitats, and the uses to which they could be applied. This put manufacturers, merchants, scientists and artisans in possession of a fixed common language in which they could speak to each other about the uses of the objects with which they dealt. As for wood, so for innumerable other categories of manufactured objects of use: tubes, wheels, wires, nails, screws, axles, bricks. This emphasis on the use-value of commodities was reiterated in the exhibitions of 1867, 1878 and 1889. The 1867 exhibition featured a Palace of Industry filled with tools, machinery and exhibits of products in various stages of manufacture, together with a History of Labour exhibit displaying tools from all eras. The 1878 exhibition highlighted the scientific discoveries of electricity and photography. The 1889 exhibition contained a Gallery of Machines, a long hall with a vaulted roof 400 feet across, where visitors, perched on a suspended walkway, could marvel at the sights and sounds of spinning wheels, clanking hammers and whirring gears.

By 1900 the aestheticised display of exchange-value had gained the upper hand. At Queen Victoria's Jubilee of 1887, the term 'spectacle', which for centuries had referred to the ceremonies by which rulers flaunted symbolic possession of their realm, could now be applied in a distinctively new sense to denote the way in which a territory was marked out by the rule of industrially manufactured signs of domination.[19] At the Paris exhibition of 1900 the decisive conjoining of material desires and imaginative desires was exemplified by the way in which the Indian exhibit at the Trocadéro was reminiscent of the Bon Marché, the first department store opened in Paris in

1852. By the time Umberto Eco visited the Montreal Exposition in 1967 the packaging was more important than the product and the aestheticisation of commodities fully installed. Noticing a pervasive oscillation between the primary function of objects, that is to say their most direct and elementary meaning, and the secondary function of objects, that is to say the way in which their mental and semantic associations shaped objects into a system of signs, Eco was led to conclude that in contemporary expositions a country no longer said 'look what I produce', but 'look how smart I am in presenting what I produce'.[20]

In the nineteenth-century exhibitions the aestheticisation of objects was *enframed*. The self-aggrandisement of those responsible for these spectacles had an irresistible proclivity to itemising lists and statistics about their swelling significance. As the exhibitions grew ever more gigantic, from exhibition to exhibition, the graph rose ever upward. The Great Exhibition of 1851 appeared colossal to contemporaries, with its 13,937 exhibitors, its 6,039,195 visitors and its 34 participating nations; but it was soon outstripped by the dramatically increased scale of the 1867 Universal Exposition in Paris, held on the Champ de Mars, which covered 41 acres; which in turn was outdone by the 1876 international exhibition of Philadelphia, with its 9,982,625 visitors and its 48-acre surface; which was then cast into the shade by the Chicago Columbian Exposition of 1904, situated on the banks of Lake Michigan, which enticed 21,477,212 visitors into its exhibition space of 580 metres. In this kind of game you cannot do better than coming top, and this the Paris Universal Exposition did in 1900, with its exhibitors and officials totalling about 9,000,000 and 48,000,000 people being lured into its elephantine extravaganza. Many visitors said they found it very hard to distinguish between the exhibition space and the rest of Paris.[21]

This, precisely, was the point: the Paris Exposition of 1900 marks the historical moment when the exhibition-value of commodities could no longer be enframed within a space apart, confined to Hyde Park or the Champs de Mars; bursting these bounds, the values

of the international exhibitions became *diffused* into the spectacle
of department stores, shopping malls, chain stores, cinemas, mail-
order houses, advertising billboards, and perpetual advertising in
newspapers, magazines, radio and television, transmuting private
and collective life into a virtually unavoidable vision of the seemingly limitless surfeit of commodities, an all-embracing medium
where people habitually interact with merchandise. No reprise of the
giganticism of 1900 would have been conceivable in the millennial
celebrations of 2000. The emphasis of the 1900 centenary within the
elephantine exhibition space which engulfed the city of Paris was
followed, a century later, in the miniaturised space of the television
screen. In a society which has perfected the semiotics of the spectacle, the origins of this ubiquitous semiotics are now scrutinised
with unprecedented erudition in the privileged site of the nineteenth-
century exhibition.[22] By the mid twentieth century Henri Lefebvre
could detect that this semiotics was a code charged with the affect of
a collective delirium in the 'consuming of displays, displays of consuming, consuming of displays of consuming, consuming of signs, and
signs of consuming'.[23] When, in agreement with this, Guy Debord, in
his *Society of the Spectacle* of 1967, pronounced that 'the entire life
in which modern conditions of production reign announces itself as
an immense accumulation of *spectacles*', he rightly saw the commodity as the focal point of all representation in capitalist societies,
a 'monopoly of appearance' which 'concentrates all gazing and all
consciousness' by presenting itself as 'something enormously positive, indisputable, and inaccessible' in a 'semiotic perpetual motion
machine'.[24]

　　In this respect the salient contrast is between contemporary
fashion and primitive sumptuary regulations. Primitive sumptuary
laws and taboos are characterised by their rigidity; and they are tied
to discriminations of social rank and hierarchy. Fashion in the contemporary west, as Jean Baudrillard and Pierre Bourdieu have elo-
quently shown, is also effective in limiting social mobility, and in
marking out the contours of social rank and nuanced discriminations.

But fashion, as distinct from sumptuary regulations, is distinguished by the illusion of total access, the assumption of a democracy of consumers and of objects of consumption; and this entails rapid turnover.[25] The consumer demands of persons in contemporary society are regulated by the criterion of 'appropriateness', which means, in effect, that the turnover rate of consumable items must be high, in contrast to the less frequent shifts in more directly regulated sumptuary systems. Just as primitive consumers are constrained by the stability of sumptuary law, so modern consumers are constrained by the velocity of fashion.

In an age when permanent and unquestioned convictions lose their former sway, life's fleeting features gain more free play, and the break with the past focusses attention on the present. The internal rhythm of persons presses for ever shorter pauses in the change of impressions – cigarettes can be smoked more rapidly than cigars – and this more impatient tempo is irresistibly drawn to temporal boundaries, to beginnings and endings, comings and goings. Fashion answers to this appeal for more frequent temporal boundaries because its diffusion annihilates the very ground of its meaning. Perched at the ever transient threshold between past and future, fashion yields, at least for as long as it enjoys its zenith, a strong sense of the present. An object is fashionable because it is in fashion at present; to remain a 'man of fashion' one must 'keep up with the times' by refurbishing one's wardrobe ceaselessly, and to write a fashionable book one must work out where the market will be in two years' time and aim for that. What is fashionable disappears as quickly as it appears; its ephemeral attractiveness incubates the seeds of its own death. In an age when fashion precipitates many transient little manufactured deaths, persons find it difficult to deal with their natural future: their own death. There is an inverse relationship between the neophilia of fashion and the taboo on speaking of death.

In his brilliant essay on fashion, Georg Simmel singles out three milieux where fashion flourishes.[26] One is the upwardly mobile middle class for whom the knowledge of inevitable death constitutes at once a rude interruption to the trajectory of a curriculum vitae and a spur to obituary-improving activities. Dominated by an unquiet temporal rhythm because their eyes are trained on the main chance, even their moment of achievement is shadowed by the slight apprehension of a possibly impending falling off should they fail to keep up their already high standards; and since the speed of their progress through life guarantees them precedence over others, they recognise in fashion the tempo of their own affective movements, as in a mirror. Another is the demi-monde, whose inclinations blatantly reveal the unacknowledged fact that the taste of their apparent opposite, the upwardly mobile, always leaves something to be desired. Consigned to the status of pariahs on account of their uprooted lifestyle, the members of the demi-monde harbour a latent resentment against all legalised, firmly existing conditions, a resentment which propels them, in their reckless embrace of what had seemed to be previously opposite choices, towards an aesthetic version – in fashion – of the drive to destroy. Finally, there is the metropolis: the disloyal speed of its swiftly changing impressions and relationships; the literal physical closeness of one person to another and the consequent code of social reserve; and the rapid upward social mobility of formerly lower strata gives them an elective affinity to rapid changes of fashion.

Fashion valorises and devalues itself simultaneously. In this it is emblematic of the category of the new which is automatically self-promoting and self-devaluing.[27] If any word has taken precedence over all others in nineteenth- and twentieth-century commodity culture, it is the word 'new'. The status of the prefix 'post' in the years following the onset of information technology was previously occupied by the adjective 'new' between the end of the Second World War and the onset of the oil crisis of 1973: with the New Realism, the New Wave, the New Criticism, the New Novel, the Nouvelle Cuisine and the New Philosophy. Already in the nineteenth century, Paul Valéry once noted, the idea of revolution anticipated this talismanic brandishing and simultaneous self-devaluation later witnessed in the ubiquity of the new: it quickly ceased to convey the idea of violent reform and became instead the expression of a wish to overturn what currently exists, whatever that may be.[28] When the enemy becomes not a particular opponent but the recent past, what matters becomes change in itself, for its own sake, the foundation of the new, which now loses any particular political foundation, being simply the compulsion to reject. Adorno, who endorsed Valéry's insight, drew the corollary that the category of the new failed to make possible any distinction between what is in fact historically new and what might appear, or be made to appear, to be new. He drew the further inference that a process of acceleration was the inevitable effect of the aesthetic of the new, resulting from its subjection to the dominance of exchange in capitalist society and the growing domination of the market over art.[29]

Given the limits to the turnover time of material goods, capitalists have turned from the production of goods to the production of services. Most goods, not by accident known as consumer durables, – knives and forks, automobiles and washing machines – have a substantial lifetime. Services and events – going to a movie or rock concert, attending health clubs – have a far shorter lifetime.[30] With this shift to the provision of services, together with the production of ephemeral objects of consumption, the turnover time of capital is accelerated. The evolution of a product from its first design and development to its eventual obsolescence – a time span referred to in marketing as the 'product life cycle' – becomes shorter. Long-term planning becomes less important, the facility to exploit market fashions more crucial. Companies innovate at a much faster rate. Advertisements flourish. Sound bites predominate. Sentences get shorter. The explicit control of time shifts attention from working time to consumption time. Punctuality as a feature of self-discipline from all members of society who want to take part in working life, the inculcation of which entailed the expenditure of so much effort in the heyday of industrialism, is now presupposed. Efforts need no longer to concentrate on the working time of human beings; it is the timetable in the life cycle of consumable products that needs to be investigated and controlled. Time control focusses on desire not discipline.[31] To ensure that production is consumed, demand must be produced, by giving meaning to commodities, by making them desirable. Whereas in an earlier phase of industrialisation the internalisation of time-discipline at work was imperative, in the present phase the internalisation of time-scheduling at consumption is required. Under the control of working time people were needed who aspired to the condition of well-oiled machines. Now they are needed to aspire to the condition of omnivorous children. As commodities are produced, desires are entrapped in commodities. To this end, a media system, capable of periodically publicising the ranking of consumable objects, is needed to organise their rapid turnover. Ranking lists of desirable objects proliferate. Only what speaks to purchasers about purchasing tends to be heard or seen or read. A radio station has an audience if it broadcasts records that sell. Immediate availability must be assured. About fifty million working Americans and their children have successfully internalised the new time discipline of consumption, which incorporates as its precondition and in a smoother form the old-time discipline of work. Their prosperity is visible in the ample houses of hundreds of suburbs, in the palatial shopping centres, in the proliferation of luxury vehicles. As a proportion of their income, consumption is at an all-time high and savings at an all-time low; borrowing at 18 per cent on a credit card to buy designer clothing is commonplace.[32] The habit of borrowing and buying becomes an addiction. Immediate availability is assured.

The desire for instantaneous availability is expressed in a whole range of technological devices and services: microwave ovens, electronic mail, fax machines, one-hour photographic development, twenty-four-hour grocery shopping. The fact that one half of all Americans are addicted to fast food is amply attested by the latest obesity statistics. In popular music the charts advertise the fact that the value of a musical object depends on the existence of alternative musical objects; the value of these musical objects rapidly vanishes once the possibility of extracting more profit from other musical objects presents itself. An object's value becomes a function of the intensity of the financial pressures exerted around the new titles waiting to enter circulation.[33] In classical music the nature of musical hearing itself changes to the extent that the unforeseen vanishes. In the process of technical reproducibility the musical work can approach technical perfectibility when sound engineering makes possible a formal reconstruction of the work in performance which excludes error, hesitation and noise. This in turn requires musical performers with new capabilities; that is, with the ability of infinitely redoing takes that are perfectible with the right sound effects. There now appears what Jacques Attali has called the virtuoso of the short phrase.[34] As in musical recording, so in book publishing: a process of historical abbreviation becomes ever more prominent. Books now go in and out of print very quickly. Previously, stocks of unsold books used to be kept for several years in a 'back-list', to supply perhaps twenty copies a year to scholars who needed them urgently. More recently, books are 'remaindered' rapidly after a short phase of full-price marketing; they are then sold off at discount in bulk; whatever remains after that is pulped. This is an efficient way of eliminating the physical embodiment of print culture discoverable earlier in publishers' back-lists.[35] All these practices exhibit the fact that usage is the public manifestation, often the display, of the velocity of financial exchange.

Consumer objects obey the pressures of increasing velocity. This acceleration effects an alienation-effect: it has been said that the past is a foreign country but now the present is becoming one too. Alvin Toffler spoke in 1970 of a 'future shock' that forces large numbers of people in western societies to live in an economic, technological and social culture alien to them because they are unable to keep up with its pace of change;[36] and now Alexander Kluge speaks of the attack of the present on the rest of time,[37] since the more the present of advanced consumer capitalism prevails over past and future the less stability or identity it provides for contemporary subjects – which is one reason, of course, why they talk about identity incessantly. Distinction in a culture of mass consumption is demonstrated by acquiring a consumer item which has just come onto the market before others acquire the same item; small time differences in the act of consumption exhibit social distinctions just as they demonstrate fine shades of physical prowess in sport. By privileging individual consumer choice the free market insinuates that all relationships, not only those between persons and consumer items, are provisional and revocable. Insofar as individuals designate themselves as members of a group, what counts is the difference of the group as a whole from what it was a year or a month before. The time of childhood too is inserted into the temporality of consumption. Benjamin, commenting in the inter-war years on the accelerated tempo of technology, as exemplified particularly in the rapid changes of fashion, observed that 'the worlds of memory replace themselves more quickly' so that 'a totally different world of memory must be set up even faster against them'.[38] Whereas the traditional and religious upbringing of earlier generations interpreted childhood dream states for them, 'the present process of childrearing boils down simply to the distraction of children'; for in a world of objects that changed its face drastically in the course of a generation, parents could no longer counsel their children, who were increasingly left to their own devices. Benjamin was prescient; childhood has now become more securely locked into the temporality of consumption. The child now learns his or her trade as a consumer, the purchase of music being a principal activity. Children no longer need to work as auxiliary factory hands; the child's labour now is to produce the consumption of music while the music industry produces the demand for it. This is, as it were, a new form of music while we work. The child thus receives an education in that most necessary activity, the drawing up of wish lists. In this way the child acquires an early training in the meaning of obsolescence: a fascination with the new which, as Andreas Huyssen has well said, includes the foreknowledge of its obsolescence in its very moment of appearance.[39] Since the ever increasing acceleration of innovation in a society oriented to profit and consumption produces ever larger quantities of soon to be obsolete objects, it follows necessarily that it must generate ever more acts of discarding. Vital to its rapid and gargantuan production of obsolescence, forgetting is an essential ingredient in the operation of the market.

3

Contemporary cultural memory is further eroded by the fate of the individual career structure. It is illuminating, in this respect, to compare the present constellation of circumstances with those typically obtaining in pre-capitalist social formations.

There, shared acts of remembering were concentrated with particular sharpness on the technical knowledge required for the accomplishment of practical skills. Whether it is a matter of blacksmiths in Africa and Asia, or trade associations in the West until the seventeenth century, the conservation of trade secrets is always at stake in acquiring apprenticeship and in sustaining the social structure of a trade.[40] Apprenticeship in craftsmanship is learned by observation. Children learn how jobs get done by observing the wheelwright, or the blacksmith, or the weaver at work; boys watch their grandfathers shooting in the woods; girls watch their grandmothers cooking, knitting, picking herbs and gardening. Among the adult population, craftsmen provide a communicational bond between members of the group, while shopkeepers act as middlemen between the village community and the world beyond. The relationships between tradesmen and buyers were conducted according to tacit rituals whose unwritten protocols guide acts of remembering and bring those acts into a kind of settled state in the shared memories of the group. For if the tradesman and the buyer are to avoid impoliteness, any excessive display of keenness in suggesting articles to purchase by the one, or in buying articles by the other, should be avoided; and if the tradesman and the buyer are to expedite their exchange as a polite human transaction it must be tacitly understood that some time should be allowed to elapse if the exchange is to be completed to the mutual satisfaction of the parties involved. These transactions require time for gossip; all encounters between buyers and sellers should be accompanied by brief verbal exchanges. All of these circumstances taken together – the acquisition of an apprenticeship, the mediating role of craftsmen and shopkeepers, the transactions of buyers and sellers – take time: time which permits acts of remembering in the group to become settled and sedimented. There is an evocation of a whole lost world of more intimate social interaction here, an evocation of what might seem somewhat romanticised. This evocation of collective memory to interpret and defend current claims often leads to historical distortion. Villagers collectively created a *remembered village* and a *remembered economy* that serve as an ideological backdrop against which to deplore the present. But it captures, nonetheless, the relative *slowness* of a social world which was as yet undriven by the imperatives of the contemporary career structure.

In industrial capitalist social formations time becomes more 'rational'. In pre-capitalist formations temporal schedules have their own kind of routines and standardisations; but in capitalist formations they became, in addition, precise, punctual, calculable, rigid, invariant and firmly coordinated.[41] This highly developed rationality of temporal scheduling is especially noticeable in the rigid sequential structure of career timetables, evident in bureaucratic procedures and in academic curricula. In the employment system of industrial capitalism generally, as it emerged in the course of the nineteenth century, standard full-time employment provides continuity based on a high degree of temporal standardisation. This standardisation was secured by the labour contract, by regular working hours in exchange for timed wages, and by particular location at the work site. The institutionalisation of the family wage – the institutional principle that a man's wage had to be high enough to support his family – closely interlinked with the development of powerful manufacturing-based unions and a male-dominated 'labour aristocracy', contributed to establishing the gender-based occupational work structure characteristic of manufacturing economies. Until well into the 1970s this system of life-long full-time work – for a long historical phase beginning at what would now be thought of as adolescence and continuing into what was then thought of as old age – was the temporal organisational model for planning and utilising labour power in the industrial plant; and it provided the organisational setting for the biographical trajectory of an individual's life.[42] Industrial institutions came to act in accordance with legally defined categories through which the standard biographies of persons were interpreted; the anatomy of the standard individual biography was given by the standard, legally defined employer–employee relationship.

The force of the standard case was exemplified by the most memorable exception to it. At the most traumatic moment in the history of capitalism, the standard work relationship which provided the mould and support for the standard individual biography began to crumble. The ground gave way: in the lives of most men and women who lived at that time the crucial economic experience of the interwar period was the cataclysmic slump of 1929 to 1933. Those whose labour was hired for wages had visited upon them unemployment on an unprecedented scale and for longer than anyone expected; nobody could remember an economic catastrophe of such dimensions in the lives of working people. The career structure which industrial capitalism had seemed to guarantee, even for the majority of the blue-collar labour force, collapsed. Between 1932 and 1933, 23 per cent of the British labour force, 27 per cent of the North American labour force, 29 per cent of the Austrian labour force and 44 per cent of the German labour force were out of a job.[43] Even when the recovery began after 1933, unemployment levels for the rest of the 1930s never fell below 16 per cent for Britain, and 20 per cent for Austria and the United States. The traumatic effect of this collapse in financial and career continuity in Central Europe, where the total disappearance of private savings left an almost complete vacuum of working capital for business, exposed the middle and lower-middle classes to the blandishments of fascism's aestheticisation of politics; while in the

United States, the epicentre of the economic earthquake, a number of photographers, Walker Evans, Dorothea Lange, Russell Lee and Arthur Rothstein, have left us with vivid visual testimony to the consequent ravages, in the lines of abandoned cars, forsaken homes and pieces of luggage, highways bordered by blown tyres, broken men and women and derelict children.

By eliminating the continuity of career structures en masse, this traumatic episode eroded trust in the capitalist system. With the exponential development of industrial capitalism, generalised trust in the institution of money had replaced the countless individual demonstrations of personal trust characteristic of pre-capitalist social formations; for anyone who places their trust in the stability of the value of money, and in the continuity of the opportunities for spending it, places their trust, not in individual people, but in the functioning of the system. If the mechanisms of industrial capitalism were to be thought viable, it had to be assumed that the money system, and the career structures dependent upon it, could reasonably enjoy trust. But during the depression of the 1930s the system no longer evidently functioned, and trust in this continuity and stability was lost.

This is why the elimination of mass unemployment was the basis of state economic policy in the countries of reformed democratic capitalism in the wake of the Second World War. In the developed world of the 1960s, Western Europe averaged 1.5 per cent of its labour force out of work, Japan 1.3 per cent. The establishment of the welfare state – the term itself only came into use in the 1940s – provided a previously unimagined safety net against the hazards of ill-health and the old age of the poor. World output in manufactures quadrupled between the early 1950s and the early 1970s; world trade in manufactured products grew tenfold during the same period. What had once been luxuries became the expected standard of comfort in the materially advanced countries: refrigerators, private washing machines, telephones. With mechanisation replacing private servants, it was possible for the average citizen to live as only the very wealthy had lived a generation earlier. The sense of historical continuity in the materially most developed parts of the world was sustained in existence all the time by the reinstallation, at a much higher level of comfort than before, of the standard individual biography within the setting of the standard employer–employee working relationship of industrial capitalism.

But with the emergence of the new informational capitalism, discontinuity, rather than continuity, became the more persuasive concept for apprehending the temporal structure of contemporary experience. The technological innovations of the Industrial Revolution had occurred in a few societies, within a limited geographical area, often isolated from other regions of the world. It took about two centuries for them to spread from their West European nucleus to the rest of the planet. Despite the process of expansion, by colonial domination in India, by commercial-industrial dependency in Latin America, by dismemberment in Africa, and by gunship diplomacy in Japan and China, this *pace of diffusion* of technologies was relatively slow by contemporary scales of measurement. Its tempo is exemplified by the diffusion of electricity. The electric telegraph was first used experimentally in the 1790s, and widely in existence from 1837; but the worldwide diffusion of electricity, which transformed transport, telegraphy, lighting and factory work schedules, dates from the 1870s. The technological innovations of the information revolution, by contrast, spread throughout the globe in less than two decades.[44] Of course, professional structural inequalities affect the access of people, regions and countries to information technology; African shanty towns, French *banlieues* and American inner cities are spatially and temporally discontinuous regions. But by the mid 1990s the hegemonic group within the worldwide division of labour were securely interlinked through an informational system which had only begun to take shape in the 1970s.

This set the historical context for the institutionalisation of casual labour markets and the pervasiveness of the temporary contract.[45] The increase in various types of part-time work, which, as much evidence shows, tends to be more lowly paid than full-time jobs, is the most general trend in the employment relationship of the service industries in developed economies. In the United States, data from the US Bureau of Labor Statistics on part-time work show that in 1989 26.1 million US workers accounting for 24 per cent of the entire national labour force were employed part-time, where part-time work means employment of between one and thirty-four hours a week. In 1988 the highest frequency of part-time work was concentrated in several major service industries: 30 per cent of all such workers were in the construction industry, while wholesale and retail industries and service industries represented, respectively, 32.5 and 38 per cent of all part-time workers; in non-agricultural industries, this amounted to a total of almost 14 million workers out of the 19.5 million part-time workers employed in non-agricultural industries. In 1988, the single largest concentration of openings was in service jobs, with part-time jobs representing 40 per cent of all openings. At about this time the US government passed legislation legitimising the use of part-time workers and creating additional incentives for employers to utilise their labour, thus further weakening the position of part-time workers. Large corporate enterprises therefore did not hesitate to utilise the principle of temporary work on a grand scale. The enormous regional telephone company Pacific Bell dismissed over 11,000 people between 1991 and 1995, and then hired 4,200 temporary contract workers by 1996, many of them their own former employees. A Labor Department study of 1995 estimated that 17 per cent of 5 million listed contract employees were working under such conditions for their former employers, such as Xerox, Delta Air Lines and Chevron. An American Management Association survey of 720 newly downsized companies demonstrated that 30 per cent had rehired the labour of their former employees, almost always without giving them back their previous health and pension benefits. The resultant personal misery was catered for by the exponential emergence of temporary help agencies which rented labour by the month, the week, or the day.

The immediate effect of informational capitalism, therefore, is to eliminate the career structure of the blue-collar labour force. Many corporate enterprises found that they could increase their turnover while eliminating personnel. Electronic automation, in the form of mechanically controlled machine tools, take over much of the productive work in the automobile, chemical and machine tool industries. Since some technical processes can be taken over entirely or in large part by robots, the new tasks of supervision, direction and maintenance can be pared down to a few highly skilled positions, and the vast number of unskilled or semi-skilled workers replaced by a small number of automation workers. Computers destroy clerical and administrative jobs by the million. Vast numbers of people, who might previously have been on the secure payrolls of state industries, or part of large bureaucracies now much reduced, or members of private businesses not enterprising enough to avoid going under, now find themselves poorly re-employed with no particular skills, or in part-time employment, or simply unemployed. At one end of the conveyor belt of technological innovation there emerge the new poor, scattered throughout the globe in the less fortunate parts of the United States and the United Kingdom, in Buenos Aires and Auckland.

This was followed by the elimination of the professional career. The shrinking temporal horizons of the great majority of the labour force could be allowed to proceed without prompting too much anxious reflection: after all, this only applied to the subaltern group, and damage to them is hardly of evident material interest to most members of the hegemonic group, particularly to those among them who have already expended so much time and energy clawing their way into membership of that group; and in any event the most eloquent written account of enormous human suffering undergone by people in some distant area of which one has no direct experience would be unlikely to cause the reader as much pain as a bite from a gnat. But a few more people begin to sit up and take notice when the institutionalisation of casual labour actually affects them. This too is a repercussion of informational capitalism: the career structures of professionals become jeopardised. While the slump of the early 1980s brought chronic insecurity into the lives of workers in manufacturing industries, the slump of the early 1990s caused large sections of the white-collar and professional classes in countries like the United States and the United Kingdom to fear that neither their jobs nor their futures were safe any longer. Some of those in less elevated positions within the worldwide informational capitalist division of labour are not well protected. High-income professional and managerial employees in many of the new specialised service and financial firms have fewer claims on their employers than had previously been the case with their equivalents in the large commercial banks and insurance houses; they are now more vulnerable to dismissal. What is commonly referred to as the greater 'flexibility' in the employment relation is a euphemistic way of saying that their jobs too have become casualised. Until the late 1980s, many large North American companies retained features typical of the post-1945 corporation: located in a particular region, they were providers of jobs to layers of managers. No longer: few USA corporations have a strong local identity, few act as members of a local community, few of them considering mass dismissals would be inhibited by the thought of community disapproval as their European or Japanese counterparts still customarily are.[46] Their attachment to a sense of place is far too tenuous for that. Through the 1990s, therefore, with the US economy booming, many famous corporations announced white-collar job eliminations, politely referred to as 'restructuring' or 're-engineering the corporation'. A great mass of not so young middle managers, forced out of their jobs, flooded the market, finding it difficult to find comparable employment elsewhere. Unsurprisingly, their distress sometimes took dramatic forms. Eight out of the ten largest mass murders in American history have occurred since 1980, typically the acts of middle-aged white men in their thirties or forties who, often after a life crisis such as losing their job or undergoing a divorce, entered a prolonged period of loneliness, frustration and rage, and finally went berserk.[47]

The casualisation of labour conditions through the institution-alisation of the temporary work contract is a historical mutation with grave repercussions because legal deregulation erodes social trust. It is true that trust, on the one hand, and a legal system, on the other, operate largely independently of one another, in the sense that we think of trust initially as a settled disposition in the relationship between persons, whereas a legal system, and herein lies both its advantage and its disadvantage, is an impersonal mechanism. Nevertheless, the very notion of trust lies at the basis of law as a whole, in the form of a generalised reliance on other people's actions; various forms of trust come into being by virtue of the limitations upon possible future risks which, officially at least, are provided by any currently operative legal regulations. Because legal arrangements give a certain measure of assurance with respect to particular expectations which persons may be disposed to entertain with regard to future contingencies that may affect them, by providing those expectations with institutional sanctions, legal arrangements form an often indispensable basis for any long-term strategic decisions and for any long-term consider-ations generally; the existence of legal regulations lessens the risk of conferring trust on particular persons because it sets any such act of trust inside the framework of legal obligations.[48]

The erosion of trust fundamentally affects the experience of time. The fact that trust takes time is illustrated vis-à-vis the past and the future. With respect to the past: because trust is hardly pos-sible without any previous information; the person who places trust in another must already be acquainted with at least certain general features, must already be to some degree informed, even if incom-pletely and unreliably, about the trustee. Trust is possible only in a familiar world; it needs history as its reliable ground. Persons tend to assume that persons and circumstances that have in the past been found to be trustworthy will continue to be so – just as those they have found to be untrustworthy will probably continue to be so –, that the familiar will remain, that if there are any signs of apparently aberrant behaviour it is probably wise to interpret them as episodic rather than typical, that what has in the past been trustworthy will most likely stand the test of time once more, and that, on the whole, the familiar will continue into the future. The fact that trust takes time is illustrated equally vis-à-vis the future: because the primary consideration is that one is going to meet again, or will most probably do so. Familiarity is the precondition for trust as well as for distrust; with respect to one's possible future relationships, it is the condition for every kind of commitment one might make towards certain persons one could encounter in the future, and it is even the foundation for our attitude, what might be called our basic ontological position, towards the future in the most general sense. In acts of trust one implicitly reduces the hypothetical complexity of the future, because in bestowing trust on persons or circumstances one commits oneself to courses of action as if there were only a certain limited set of possibilities in the future. Trust is the essential ingredient in expectations of historical continuity, expectations which yield guidelines for the conduct of our everyday life.

With the institutionalisation of casualised labour and the increasing pervasiveness of the temporary work contract, the reality of the labour market has long since rendered the traditional idea of a more or less continuous, predominantly male, working life, recompensed by the timed wage or salary, obsolete. The decline of manufacturing-based unions, the large-scale displacement of male workers, the growth of part-time work and the growth in the numbers of female-headed households: all these circumstances have combined to erode the institution of the family wage, which was an intrinsic component of the employer–employee relationship under the legal regulations of industrial capitalism. What was previously the standard individual biography – in tandem with the often silenced biography of one half of the human race –, which was legally locked into the work relationship of industrial capitalism, is passé. In the foreseeable future, this type of standard biography, even if it is conceivable that there may be any such thing, is likely to be accessible only to a small group of the gainfully employed.[49] With the disappearance of the standard biography encased in the previously standard employer–employee relationship, the sense of time, as institutionally structured and personally experienced, is fundamentally altered; and along with this, with respect to the whole context of individual life trajectories, culturally specific acts of remembering and forgetting are altered.

With the elimination of the standard individual biography the metanarrative of History comes to be fractured, if not eliminated, too. This is hardly surprising. How the narratives of individual persons are experienced and conceived of affects the way in which the course of historical events generally is experienced and conceived. Both are predicated on trust, or its absence. That faith in History as a grand metanarrative began to erode as the 1970s passed into the 1980s is no historical coincidence: for the metanarrative of historical progress was dependent in part for its plausibility on the existence of stable individual career structures, and the sense of time grounded in them, which ensured continuity in the lives of so many individuals. In the boom post-war years, from the slow recovery after 1945 until the economic crisis of the mid 1970s, the faith in economic, technical and individual progress were structurally interlinked and reciprocally reinforcing. Great increase in economic productivity and technological innovation led, at the time, to a general democratisation of previously exclusive standards of living, based all the while on what appeared to be the solid foundation of the industrial career structure. It was this, at least in part, which buoyed up the continuing background belief in some sort of metanarrative of History, for if the trauma of the Depression was unforgettable for those who had experienced it personally, it could be consigned to the domain of historical ignorance by most of those who had not.

It appears to have required the fall-out from the transformation from industrial to informational capitalism for doubts about the credibility of a *metanarrative* of History to be unashamedly proclaimed and, in some quarters, celebrated. In *La condition postmoderne*, Jean-François Lyotard termed postmodern the collapse of belief in the great narrative of humanity's emancipation and securement of freedom, that unifying narrative grounded in the Enlightenment's discourse of progress that had for two centuries legitimated knowledge. When Jürgen Habermas endorsed Lyotard's report by seeing the catchword of postmodernity as the rejection of modern reason since the Enlightenment, he also diverged from him in warning of the grievous repercussions entailed by the fact that postmodernism was identified with a political and social neo-conservatism. For postmodernism, being an absence of faith in the future, also causes the past to lose its historicity, by reducing it to a repertoire of contextless and arbitrarily exploitable forms. Habermas' reply to Lyotard therefore underlined the fact that what is involved in the debate is not a matter of discourse alone: the life histories of countless individuals are involved, not just the careers of those who produce texts about discourses.[50] The increasing structural disparity between the hegemonic and the subaltern group within the worldwide division of labour of informational capitalism has eroded both stable career structures and historical metanarratives – the sense of temporality, in both cases, being grounded in the experience of, or in the absence of, both historical continuity and cultural trust. Once again, the sense of history becomes abbreviated, cultural memory effaced. We face a large-scale ironic reversal: the increasing life expectancy of persons' lives is undercut by the shrinking life expectancy of their careers. What is remembered becomes ever more obsolete with respect to its specific applicability to the life experience of work.

4

The temporality of consumption is evidently implicated in a further temporality, and one which is central to the way we experience structures of temporality in our culture, that of the media. If we are confronted by endless sea-tides of verbal and visual and acoustic waste matter, a pervasively swelling 'noise' which abbreviates our scale of time and induces cultural forgetting, this is in large measure due to the imbrication of consumption time and media time, in the context of which three media forms might be singled out: the newspaper, television and information technology. Historically, these modes of communication have competed with one another; and the gradual replacement of older forms of narration by information, and of information by sensation, is a repercussion of this innovative competition, the results of which, while apparently extending our repertoire of choice, actually atrophy our human experience.[51] The current preoccupation with memory is surely, paradoxically, in part a concerted effort of cultural discarding, an attempt to *slow down* the processes of this communicative burden, by retrieving a mode of reflection outside and in opposition to the world of accelerated informational overload.

To begin this story of media supersession with the newspaper is, in a sense, to start the narrative at a stage too late, since newsprint realises a potentiality already contained in the printed book. In his *Évolution de la mémoire* of 1910, Henri Pieron spoke of the printing press as the machine which permitted 'the fantastic acceleration of mnemonic progress in modern societies by multiplying the prints and traces of memory':[52] a typographical memory of events which, in principle, made possible, by its very invention, an increasingly multiplied quantity of printed words. However numerous and spatially dispersed they may be, the readers of a printed text share an identical object. The silent communication system of printing permits the book to anticipate the newspaper in the way in which it gives rise to a historically new sense of a set of invisible interactions all occurring at once.[53] But although newspapers were widely diffused in Europe by the end of the eighteenth century, it would be misleading to read off from this fact the modern sense of rapid social action at a distance to which mass circulation newspapers have accustomed us. Before the mid nineteenth century newspapers were still too expensive to allow for mass readership. Because of their relative rarity, newspapers were read in cafés. Otherwise they could be obtained only by subscription; in 1824 the twelve most widely distributed newspapers in France had altogether about 56,000 subscriptions. Weighty

political considerations came into play here: the liberals as well
as the royalists were interested in keeping the lower classes away
from newspapers. In any event, such strategic concerns were con-
veniently accommodated by the then limits of technological possibility.[54] In 1792 there were thirteen daily newspapers in London, in
1779 there were thirty-five newspapers in Paris. Yet news of the fall
of the Bastille in 1789 took thirteen days to reach Madrid; the victory
at Trafalgar on 21 October 1805 was not reported in London until
2 November; a London newspaper created a record by announcing
the victory at Waterloo in 1815 – 240 miles away – four days after the
battle, but it took nearly two months for London to receive news of
Napoleon's death, about the same period required to transmit news of
Nelson's victory on the Nile. This is an entirely different world from
that inhabited by Keynes in 1921 when, referring to the enormous
influence of the popular newspapers on the various positions taken
up by Lloyd George and Briand in the Paris talks on war reparations,
he pointed to what he took to be the unprecedented circumstance
in which the most powerful and intelligent statesmen were com-
pelled by inescapable forces to meet together day by day to discuss
detailed variations of the impossible. What he meant by his reference to 'inescapable forces' was the nature of the mass audience as
an environment, the ability to conduct mass persuasion through the
new mechanical method which had recently turned public opinion
into the raw material of political life.

It was the mass production of newspapers, with millions of
copies of a single issue printed overnight, that made this possible.[55]
This is a phenomenon of the twentieth century. A British newspaper
reached a million-copy sale for the first time only in the 1890s, a
French one around 1900. For this to be possible two developments
were indispensable, one organisational, the other technological.
Organisationally, it was the emergence of news agencies that altered
the scope of news dissemination. The founding of Havas in 1835,
of Wolff's in 1849 and of Reuters in 1851 led on, within a decade,
to the first agreement between them on the delimitation of sources

and markets and on the exchange of news. More important still were developments in printing technology. The printing press of the eighteenth century had been little different from that used by Gutenberg some centuries earlier. It consisted of a wooden hand-press – wood was later replaced by metal – on which a flat plate was laid upon a flat piece of paper with pressure being created by the tightening of screws. The invention of the cylinder introduced a radically new method of printing: in the double rotary cylinder of the 1850s a curved plate wound about the cylinder could print two sides of a piece of paper at once; by the 1890s octuple rotary presses were capable of printing 96,000 copies of eight pages in an hour as against the average of 2,500 an hour of seventy years earlier. Modern typesetting techniques also affected velocity: the linotype developed by Mergenthaler and put onto the market in 1886 quintupled the speed of typesetting. What is remarkable is the long delay between the point at which the principle of simultaneity inherent in newsprinting makes its first appearance and the point at which it becomes fully effective with the mass circulation of newsprint.

The idea of the simultaneous, as Benedict Anderson has demonstrated,[56] is built into both the conventions and the circulation of the newspaper. The composition of the broadsheet newspaper confronts the reader on its first page with five or more diverse reported events. A story about civil disorder in Russia, a war in Kosovo, a massacre in East Timor, an emotive bit of speech acting by Clinton, a murder and a football match: most of these events occur independently without the actors having much awareness of what the others are up to. At once an anticipation and perpetuation of the artistic practice of montage introduced by the historical avant-garde, and a structured experience of confusion which reflects the modern metropolis' shattering of experience into fragments at work and leisure, the newspaper trains its readers in the scanning and apprehension of detailed and decontextualised 'articles' whose associative connection is constituted through additive juxtaposition of discrete elements. It is calendrial coincidence – the date at the

head of the newspaper – that provides the imagined linkage between
the constituent elements, the subtext being that all juxtaposed items
are emplotted inside the grid of a quantifiably homogeneous time
within whose frame 'the world' moves on. As American newscasters
used to reiterate during the period of the Cold War: 'time marches
on'. The idea of simultaneity is built too into the circulation of the
newspaper, which requires simultaneous transmission to people who
must know that this information will be obsolete on the day after its
printing. When Hegel said that the reading of the daily newspaper
is modern man's version of morning prayer, he foresaw the emergence of a new ritual whose participants, in ceremonial repetition
at daily intervals throughout the calendar, know that their own act
of consumption is being replicated by thousands, perhaps millions,
of others. But where Hegel foresaw the role of newspapers as a modern ritual, Benjamin saw that this was a ritual which, unlike traditional forms, precipitated not memory reinforcement through the
re-echoing of earlier repetitions, but memory loss: in the sense that
the principles of journalistic reportage – freshness of news, brevity,
rapid comprehensibility, disconnection between discrete items – iso-
late what is reported to have happened from the sphere in which it
could deeply enter into the affective experience, and so the affective
time, of readers.[57]

This amnesiac effect is potentiated by the daily exposure to a
multiplication of televisual images. The diffusion of television takes
place in a television environment, where objects and symbols – the
shapes of home furniture, acting styles, conversational themes – are
incessantly self-referential. Television is not a set but a setting, for all
processes that are communicated, in politics, business, sport and art.
In advanced societies politicians who are not on television stand no
chance of obtaining people's support, since electronically based communication *is* communication as such. Attempts have been made to
quantify this almost constant background presence.[58] The average
American home, it was calculated in the late 1980s, had a television
set on for about 7 hours a day, actual viewing being estimated at 4.5

daily hours per adult. The weekly average of television watching time was quantified with finer exactitude for Japan in 1992 as 8 hours 17 minutes per day. Not all materially advanced countries achieve such high levels of spectatorship; it appears that in the late 1980s, French adults watched television only about 3 hours a day, presumably having their minds on other things. Even when a healthy douche of scepticism has been poured over these quantitative estimates, it remains reasonable to suppose that in urban societies media consumption is the second largest category of waking time behind work. But mere quantity of attention, or relative inattention, is less important than the fact that all televisual messages are integrated into a common cognitive pattern. When interactive educational programmes look like video games, when newscasts are constructed like audio-visual shows, and when trial cases are screened like soap operas, it is evident that different modes of communication are borrowing codes from each other.[59]

A culture's memory cannot remain unaffected by this codification. Max Weber argued that the effect of instrumental rationality was the disenchantment of the world; the effect of the television environment is its dematerialisation. The telespectator has no material object to watch or possess, only the experience of watching fleeting images on the screen. In the transient immateriality of this communication solid matter evaporates. The concept of the enduring becomes ethereal. The accelerated perspectival shifts of adroit camera work mean that, in place of the passive perspective of painting which permits elaborate and careful scrutiny, the telespectator becomes habituated to the experience of vertigo, a flexible optical velocity which has been compared with the eye-popping view one can experience when bungee-jumping. The telespectator can easily accelerate these perspectival shifts further by the routine procedure of 'flipping through channels', juxtaposing disjunct times and spaces in a virtual simultaneity where the perception of history appears as infinite distraction by an endless reserve of equal events. The promiscuous exposure to nervous stimuli described by

Simmel in his great essay on 'The Metropolis and Mental Life' of 1900 as characteristic of the modern city dweller begins to seem sedate by comparison. Culturally institutionalised forgetting is necessarily entailed because for the telespectator the past, the most immediate past included, becomes an evanescent collection of images whose transmission, far from reinforcing, actually weakens the links between personal experience and public memory. Partly this is because of the assemblage of images: history, as narrative, is first organised according to the availability of visual materials, then submitted to the possibility of selecting seconds of frames to be pieced together, or spliced apart, such that the overall effect, in news reports as in advertising, is of a non-continuous, non-sequential temporality. And partly this is because of the sheer surfeit of images: informational overload is one of the best devices for forgetting, the function of the news media being not to produce, nor even to consume, but rather to discard, to consign recent historical experience to oblivion as rapidly as possible.

Telespectators perceive abbreviated time because the time element previously dependent on spatial distance in reporting information shrinks. News events are reported not as they had been witnessed but as they are being witnessed. The birth of vicarious visual witness was roughly contemporaneous with the early history of aviation. A tragic aeroplane accident took place in December 1910, resulting in the deaths of the aviators Laffont and Mariano Pola, when 'the Gaumont company was able to film the crash of the aviators second by second and a few hours after the accident the Gaumont theatre situated on the Paris boulevards projected fifty minutes of film reproducing the tragic event'.[60] There now exists a hyperspace of representation in which everyone is already technically in possession of the instantaneous reproduction of their own life. A cluster of world-historical events have now naturalised the activity of virtual witnessing. The disaster at the nuclear plant in Chernobyl was swiftly photographed by a French commercial satellite, and then transmitted all over the world, including within the Soviet Union itself.[61]

The Chinese government's suppression of the students in Tiananmen Square in 1989, and the outside world's shock at that event, were immediately reported back into China by television, fax messages and radio.[62] With the cascading collapse of the Communist regimes in Eastern Europe in late 1989, pictures of each government's demise led to similar events in neighbouring states. The collapse of the Soviet state in August 1991 could be watched minute by minute in real time, with simultaneous translation of Russian political debates.[63]

The activity of consigning information to oblivion is nowhere more highly developed than in those devices which stockpile information most effectively: that is, in those technologies of information processing and communication which converge around microelectronics, computing, telecommunications/broadcasting and optoelectronics, which, taken together, have since the 1980s brought about the decisive process of transformation currently shaping the world of informational capitalism. Its time unit is the nanosecond. Tracy Kidder quotes the words of an engineer for whom the new time frame has become naturalised. 'It's funny', the engineer says, 'I feel very comfortable talking in nanoseconds. I sit at one of these analysers and nanoseconds are *wide*. I mean, you can see them go by. "Jesus", I say, "that signal takes twelve nanoseconds to get from there to there". Those are real big things to me when I'm building a computer. Yet when I think about it, how much longer it takes to snap your fingers, I've lost track of what a nanosecond really means.'[64] The snapping of the fingers takes about half a second: in human time it is just barely perceptible; in computer time it is 500 million nanoseconds. To note this fact is to establish that instantaneity is a fiction; even the time of rapid perception takes time. But this 'taking time' is now accomplished with such velocity that for business leaders, the introduction of devices such as telex, fax, electronic mail and computerised book-keeping have produced a global space in which information is circulated among physically remote places such as New York, Tokyo and London such that changes or adaptations immediately ricochet around the whole network rather than remaining within the temporal and spatial isolation of a particular local environment; while for average consumers instant computerised access to products, services and data are available, from ordering replacement parts for electric household devices, or scheduling express-mail pick-up, or checking credit card balance, or researching flight tickets, or retrieving bibliographic information. Though instantaneity is a fiction, the transfer of huge quantities of information virtually without time delay is a commonplace.

A less immediately evident effect of information technology, but one no less important, is the alteration of cultural memory. The disturbing premonition that the human sensorium was becoming overloaded by excess information which might precipitate maladies of forgetting long predated the invention of the computer. Henri Pieron, who had established an international reputation as an experimental psychologist with his *Évolution de la mémoire*, warned in 1910 that one effect of the machine age was the trauma of too much information, 'One risks losing oneself – one almost begins to wish for the ancient destructive amnesias of the fire at the celebrated library of Alexandria.'[65] What was for him an almost acknowledged wish has long become a *fait accompli*. The routinisation of computer processing necessarily entails amnesias. There now exists a generation of Japanese young people who have developed previously unknown cognitive capabilities lacking in the older generation, even though the latter may have already grown up with computers; they are able to watch several programmes on computer screens simultaneously and to grasp the narrative structures.[66] Sherry Turkle describes the psychostructure of young computer freaks who, through interaction with technology, create their own temporal world largely isolated from the social events around them.[67] Raymond Barglow compares the classic dreams reported in Freud's writing with his own patients' dreams in the high tech environment of 1990s San Francisco, when the latter's novelty consists in the dreamer's sense of absolute solitude, a solitude experienced as existential and inescapable, built into the structure of the world.[68] Though extreme, these cases are culturally symptomatic.

By accelerating time, computer usage immerses individuals in a hyper-present, an intensified immediacy which, by training the viewer's attention on a rapid succession of micro-events, makes it ever more difficult to envisage even the short-term past as 'real', since the present comes to be experienced as a narrowly defined time-period unlinked from past causes. Perhaps it is no accident that the term 'linkage' acquired such prominence in public discourse about the time of the Gulf War: it marks an already felt lack. For when such a present forces itself on the attention of individuals and increasingly on large parts of whole societies, it become ever harder, not just to entertain the credibility of metanarratives, but even to conceive of any long-term historical coherence. Cultural memory is effaced.

The onset of forgetting and the longing for the moment proceed in tandem. An insidious oppression invades the lives of people who, while they concentrate on one piece of information, are forever subliminally reminded that they are losing the possibility of concentrating fully, or even just attending peripherally, to another item of information. Sharp in the background is the thought that they might be in other places, or with other men, or other women, or at other meetings, or at other exhibitions, or reading other books, or pursuing other goals. People now incessantly talk about 'the other', yet they rarely mention the fact that among these others that tweak at their peripheral vision are the other ways in which they might be spending their time. This sense of lacking time can assume panic proportions. People can have the feeling of having just missed this, or that, or the other. They long for the moment; but even the moment dissolves into an array of hypothetical moments. The more effectively their consciousness screens off the bombardment of stimuli, the less these impressions enter into their affective experience, tending to remain, as Benjamin once put it, in the sphere of a certain hour of one's life, so that, in assigning to an incident a precise point in time in consciousness, people turn that incident into merely a moment that has been lived. Impoverishment of affect brings exorbitance of cynicism. Exposed to what Debord has called the 'diffuse spectacle' – that which the spectacle ceases to speak of for three days, he has argued, no longer exists – they find historical knowledge annihilated, the recent past in particular destroyed, as the reign of a perpetual present is installed in its place. Affective time becomes thinned out, as time schedules become thickened. Present time is packed to bursting point; past time is evacuated.

5

Whether we are dealing with the labour process, or consumption, or career structures, or media production, we are concerned, to be sure, with different *types* of forgetting. Nonetheless, taken together as an ensemble, the temporality of the labour process, the temporality of consumption, the temporality of the career structure, and the temporality of media production, all precipitate a cascade of reciprocally reinforcing repercussions the overall effect of which is to install *systemic forgetting* into the structure of modernity itself.

As it happens, none of these temporal structures are intelligible without constant reference to a certain number of quite palpable and self-evident entities with which we are familiar in everyday life. Again and again we have encountered the manufactured objects of modernity: knives, forks, washing machines, automobiles, advertisements, shopping centres, microwave ovens, fax machines, popular and classical musical records, publishers' booklists, newspapers, television sets, newsreel cameras, computers. Implicitly *the whole object-world* of modernity has been all the time within the range of our attention. All these objects, this whole object-world, is situated within life-spaces which have become for us routine; and there is something recognisably characteristic about places that we think of as modern, something culturally specific about the way in which modernity has gone about the task of socially producing its spaces. To the cluster of interlocking processes we have just passed in review, whose temporalities have set in motion a powerful and pervasive structured forgetting, we therefore need to add at least one related element: the topography of modern urban space.

On the matter of modern topography, one observation is self-evident. Place, at least in one sense in which that word is understood, is less and less a determining fact of our lives. The conquest over the tyranny of distance has helped to free people from the accident of location. We are no longer rooted in one place, as farmers were for many generations. Physical separation, even though it may be attended by separation anxieties, is no longer, as it was even a century and a half ago, a kind of little death. The accident of the place where we are born no longer determines, to anything like the extent it previously did, the job we take, the friends we have and the places where we shop. Automobiles, aeroplanes, radio, television, telephones, satellites, cables and computers, all cause us increasingly to experience whatever place we are in as a place we *happen* to occupy or may want to exchange for another. Place is no longer felt as the force of destiny. It is as likely to signify rootlessness: a rootlessness, or loss of place, built into the suburban landscape with its jumble of supermarkets, hamburger joints and criss-crossing highways. Our life-spaces bear the marks of mobility rather than locatedness. At the lower end of the labour market, certain mobilities are coerced, the movement of people who must leave home in order to survive, and whose movements are organised within régimes of dependent labour, so that what emerges are new demographic mappings: borderland ethnicities unevenly assimilated to dominant nation-states. At the upper end of the labour market, mobility acquires the meaning of mental as well as physical fitness; willingness for professional mobility is regarded as a prerequisite for even remaining in the labour market, and, adroitly managed, mobility is a precondition for advancement in a successful career.

This slow supersession of locatedness by mobility was accompanied in the long history of modernity by a sequence of more or less observable, and more or less obtrusive, shocks, to which we have now long become naturalised. In his essay 'A Plea for Gas Lamps', Robert Louis Stevenson, lamenting the fact that, with the disappearance of gas lanterns, the cushioning effect of slowly descending darkness had become an almost inaccessible experience, reflected on the rhythm with which lamplighters had previously gone through the streets and lit one lantern after another; on how at first this rhythm contrasted with the uniform onset of the dusk, and on how later those who had been familiar with this old practice experienced as disturbing the new contrast with the brutal shock caused by the spectacle of entire cities suddenly being illuminated by electric light.[69] This precipitate electrical illumination had its miniature analogue in the 'snapping' of the photographer, when the touch of a finger sufficed to fix an event for an unlimited period of time. While in the cinema, perception in the form of mild shocks was established as a formal principle, the tactile experience of snapping photographs was joined by the optic experience of the kind solicited by the advertising pages of a newspaper. Moving through traffic also habituated individuals to a series of minor shocks, as they were obliged to cast glances in all directions in order not to miss traffic signals; at dangerous crossings, as Benjamin wrote of the urban pedestrian, 'nervous impulses flow through him in rapid succession, like the energy through a battery'. This visual wariness was compounded by exposure to new kinds of noise. Noise control was implemented in relation to the automobile, whose noise was initially perceived as a form of violence. Article 25 of the legislative decision of the French Government on 31 December 1911 made sounding one's horn a duty, but added that 'in densely populated areas, the volume of the sound emitted by the horn shall remain low enough that it does not inconvenience the residents and passers-by. The use of multiple-sounding horns, sirens, and whistles is prohibited.'[70]

The term noise is now commonly used not only of acoustic disturbances but, in an extended usage, as a technical term signifying any form of interference with meaningful messages. In principle, then, it can refer to visual and even tactile as well as acoustic phenomena. Noise was always associated with thoughts of destruction, disorder, dirt and pollution; and in modern information theory the term noise is used to refer to a signal that interferes with the reception of a message by a receiver, even if the interfering message itself has a meaning for that receiver. With respect to acoustic noise in particular, it is known that the consequence of excessive sound in the environment is diminished intellectual capacity, accelerated respiration and heartbeat, hypertension, and slowed digestion.[71] With respect to metropolitan noise understood more generally, Valéry long ago observed the inclination to recoil: the inhabitants of the great urban centres, he wrote, revert to a state of savagery – that is, of isolation. The feeling of being dependent on others, which used to be kept alive by need, is gradually blunted in the smooth functioning of the social mechanism. Any improvement of this mechanism eliminates certain modes of behaviour and emotions.[72]

Yet this inclination to recoil from the new sensory field of metropolitan noise of which Valéry speaks had its counterpole in what might be called the euphoria of the momentary. The number and variation of relationships in the new spaces of the giant city, and the fleetingness and superficiality of interaction that was becoming habitual there, led also to a new evaluation of the momentary, to a sense of the unbounded charm of the moment. The brevity and infrequency of meetings which were now being allotted to each individual, compared with the more leisurely interactions characteristic of life in a small town, made it necessary to come to the point as quickly as possible and to make as striking an impression as one could in the briefest possible time. This euphoria of the momentary was displayed on a massive scale at the Paris exhibition of 1900. Within the same exhibitionary space there were to be found reproductions of the most disparate places: an incongruous jumble of Hindu temples, pagodas, Algerian alleys, Chinese, Japanese and Senegalese quarters. Twenty-one of the thirty-three major attractions at the exposition involved the dynamic illusion of a voyage.[73]

It is hardly surprising, then, that this new experiential field entailed what Valéry called the elimination of certain modes of behaviour and emotion. Prominent among these modes of behaviour and emotion which are slowly eliminated, as we can now see, are certain capacities of what Proust called voluntary memory. The opening pages of *À la recherche du temps perdu*, as is well known, are concerned to clarify the distinction between voluntary memory and involuntary memory. The distinguishing feature of voluntary memory is that it is at the service of the intellect. Proust's narrator tells us how poorly, for many years, he remembered the town of Combray, in which he had spent part of his childhood; and how, one afternoon, the taste of a madeleine transported him back to the past, whereas until then he had been limited to the promptings of a memory which obeyed the call of conscious *attentiveness*. This memory prompted by attentiveness, which Proust terms 'mémoire volontaire', had as its characteristic that the information which it gives us about the past retains no trace of that past. Proust is insistent upon this. 'It is the same', he writes, 'with our own past. In vain we try to conjure it up again; the efforts of our intellect are futile.' The past, by which he here means our autobiographical past drenched with affect, Proust says, 'is somewhere beyond the reach of the intellect' – that is to say, of the voluntary memory – 'and unmistakably present in some material object (or in the sensation which such an object arouses in us)'.[74]

Yet if voluntary memory, which obeys the promptings of our conscious attentiveness, yields a meagre harvest because it is incapable of giving access to the deeper affective layers of our autobiographical past, it is surely all the more historically significant that even *voluntary* memory was coming to be thought problematic and limited by some of Proust's contemporaries. Not by chance were the psychological theories of the late nineteenth century so intensively preoccupied with the problem of perception, of duration and of the traces which every temporal perception left behind in the memory.[75] Some of the experimental psychological work on the nature of attention was the achievement of James McKeen Cattell, whose experiments on students at the University of Columbia provided the classical data for the notion of *range of attention*; as early as 1910, hundreds of experimental laboratory studies had been completed specifically on the range of attention in advertising. From the 1890s until well into the 1930s, one of the central themes of experimental psychology was the nature of attention: that is, on the relation between stimulus and attention, and on the problems of concentration, focalisation and distraction. How many sources of stimulation, the experimental psychologists kept asking, could one attend to simultaneously? The key position of these questions in the discourse of experimental psychology surfaced at precisely the time – between the 1890s and the 1930s – when there emerged a social field increasingly saturated with sensory input: that is to say, the urban topography of the giant city.

The cityscape, like the screen, is saturated with images, its physical sense of space decomposed as our eyes are continuously exposed to flooding acoustic and optical impressions, overheard and glimpsed as if in constant flight, and so making it difficult for us to sustain a belief in a reality which might be either stable or permanent. If we want to gauge the exponential development of this optical and acoustic bombardment, we might first recall Benjamin's response, three-quarters of a century ago, to the excessive nervous stimuli of city streets which, in their relative novelty, he perceived as optical projectiles hurtling at the spectators' sensorium so that the mind registered them as so many shock experiences; and we might then juxtapose that reflective reaction of the 1930s with the experience we now have when we watch old films, those produced during Benjamin's lifetime or even later still, which when they show scenes shot in the street often appear to us unfamiliar, spare and stripped of encumbrances, lacking as they do that array of signs, the numerous traffic lights, the roundabouts, the roadmarkings regulating lanes and parking, which we now take for granted. The effect of this progressive multiplication of cityscape images, this ever more exorbitant frenzy of the visible,[76] is, if not to annihilate historical knowledge, then at least to corrode and consume the recent past.

The investigation of forgetting, as a systematic contemporary cultural phenomenon, thus leads us ultimately and inevitably to the problem of *place*, and, more specifically still, to the question of place memory. But to investigate place memory in more detail we need to take a large step backwards: a step of some two thousand years.

NOTES

1. On working time see E. P. Thompson, 'Time, work-discipline, and industrial capitalism', *Past and Present*, 38 (1967), pp. 56–97.
2. K. Marx, *Grundrisse: Foundations of the Critique of Political Economy* (Eng. tr. New York, 1973), pp. 360–1.
3. On the idea of a 'general human signature' see E. Scarry, *The Body in Pain* (New York and Oxford, 1985), pp. 311–14.
4. G. Lukács, *History and Class Consciousness* (Eng. tr. Cambridge, Mass., 1971), pp. 83–222. On the transformation of the diachronicity of the labour process into the illusory synchronicity of exchange value see G. Cohen, *Karl Marx's Theory of History: A Defence*, appendix 1 (Princeton, 1978).
5. See C. Ginzburg, 'Clues: roots of an evidential paradigm', in *Myths, Emblems, Clues* (London, 1990), pp. 96–125.
6. F. Moretti, 'Clues', in *Signs Taken for Wonders* (Chicago, 1983), pp. 130–56.
7. W. Cronon, *Nature's Metropolis: Chicago and the Great West* (New York and London, 1991).
8. R. Williams, *The Country and the City* (New York, 1973).
9. E. Weber, *Peasants into Frenchmen: The Modernization of Rural France 1870–1914* (London, 1977).
10. E. Renan, *Qu'est-ce qu'une nation?* (Paris, 1882).
11. D. Harvey, *Justice, Nature and the Geography of Difference* (Cambridge, Mass., 1996), pp. 306–10.
12. S. Toulmin, *The Philosophy of Science* (London, 1953), pp. 121–3.
13. M. de Certeau, *The Practice of Everyday Life* (Berkeley, 1984), pp. 121 ff.
14. H. Jonas, 'The nobility of sight: a study in the phenomenology of the senses', in *The Phenomenon of Life: Toward a Philosophical Biology* (Chicago, 1982); R. Rorty, *Philosophy and the Mirror of Nature* (Princeton, 1979).

15. M. Horkheimer and T.W. Adorno, *Dialectic of Enlightenment* (Eng. tr. New York, 1972), p. 230.

16. G. Debord, *Society of the Spectacle* (Eng. tr. Detroit, 1977).

17. R. Brain, *Going to the Fair: Readings in the Culture of Nineteenth-Century Exhibitions* (Cambridge, 1993), p. 14.

18. Ibid., pp. 73–4, 77–9.

19. T. Richards, *The Commodity Culture of Victorian England. Advertising and Spectacle 1851–1914* (Stanford, 1990), p. 113.

20. U. Eco, 'A theory of expositions' (1967), quoted in Brain, *Going to the Fair*, p. 196.

21. On the exponential development in the size of nineteenth-century exhibitions see Brain, *Going to the Fair*, pp. 9–10.

22. For studies of nineteenth-century exhibitions see in particular: R. W. Rydell, *The Books of the Fairs: A Guide to World Fair Historiography* (Chicago, 1992); B. Schroeder-Gudehus and A. Rasmussen, *Les fastes du progrès: le guide des expositions universelles 1851–1992* (Paris, 1992); J. Allwood, *The Great Expositions* (London, 1977); J. Findling, ed., *Historical Dictionary of World's Fairs and Expositions, 1851–1983* (New York, 1990); P. Greenhalgh, *Ephemeral Vistas: The Expositions Universelles, Great Exhibitions, and World's Fairs 1851–1939* (Manchester, 1988); R. D. Mandell, *Paris 1900: The Great World's Fair* (Toronto, 1967); R. Mainardi, *Art and Politics of the Second Empire: The Universal Exposition of 1855 and 1867* (New Haven and London, 1987); P. Ory, *Les expositions universelles de Paris* (Paris, 1982); R. Williams, *Dream Worlds: Mass Consumption in Late Nineteenth-Century France* (Berkeley and Los Angeles, 1982).

23. H. Lefebvre, *Everyday Life in the Modern World* (Eng. tr. New York, 1973), p. 90.

24. Debord, *Society of the Spectacle*, p. 39.

25. A. Appadurai, ed. *The Social Life of Things: Commodities in Cultural Perspective* (Cambridge, 1986); on sumptuary laws see pp. 21, 22, 25, 31–3, 38–9, 57.

26. G. Simmel, 'Die Mode', in *Philosophische Kultur* (Potsdam, 1923), pp. 31–64.

27. On this feature of the category of the 'new' see generally A. Compagnon, *The 5 Paradoxes of Modernity* (Eng. tr. New York, 1994).

28. See ibid., p. 62.

29. Ibid., p. 60.

30. On the speeding-up of the turnover time of capital see D. Harvey, *The Condition of Postmodernity* (Oxford, 1990), pp. 182, 210–11, 229–31, 240, 266, 270–1, 284–5, 343.

31. J. Attali, *Noise: The Political Economy of Music* (Eng. tr. Minneapolis, 1985), p. 130.

32. E. Luttwak, *Turbo-Capitalism: Winners and Losers in the Global Economy* (London, 1998), p. 206.

33. Attali, *Noise*, p. 130.

34. Ibid., p. 106.

35. Luttwak, *Turbo-Capitalism*, p. 231.

36. A. Toffler, *Future Shock* (New York, 1970).

37. A. Huyssen, *Twilight Memories: Marking Time in a Culture of Amnesia* (New York and London, 1995), p. 26.

38. W. Benjamin, *Gesammelte Schriften*, 6 vols. ed. R. Tiedemann and H. Schweppenhäuser (Frankfurt, 1972–), vol. v, pp. 596, 490, 118, 1214.

39. Huyssen, *Twilight Memories*, p. 26.

40. A. Leroi-Gourhan, *Le geste et la parole*, vol. ii: *La mémoire et les rythmes* (Paris, 1964–5), p. 66.

41. On the standardisation of time see H. Nowotny, *Time: The Modern and Postmodern Experience* (Eng. tr. Cambridge, 1994), pp. 18, 22, 24–5, 37.

42. On industrialisation and family life see U. Beck, *Risk Society: Towards a New Modernity* (Eng. tr. London, 1992), pp. 104–5, 106–10, 114, 119–21.

43. On inter-war unemployment see E. Hobsbawm, *Age of Extremes: The Short Twentieth Century 1914–1991* (London, 1994), pp. 89–90, 92–4.

44. M. Castells, *The Rise of the Network Society* (Cambridge, Mass., 1996), pp. 33, 38–9.

45. On the casualisation of work see S. Sassen, *The Global City: New York, London, Tokyo* (Princeton, 1991), pp. 33, 238–43, 249, 280, 282, 300, 306, 314–15, 317–19, 337. On the mass unemployment resulting from informational capitalism see U. Beck, *Risk Society: Towards a New Modernity* (Eng. tr. London, 1992), pp. 13, 88–9, 111, 120, 124, 134, 140–2, 145–6, 149, 223, 224–5, 230; and Hobsbawm, *Age of Extremes*, pp. 304, 406, 413–15.

46. P. Kennedy, *Preparing for the Twenty-First Century* (London, 1994), p. 58.

47. 'Unstable jobs, even if truly well-paid, are not qualitatively the same as stable, career jobs; they only sustain immediate consumption, not the building-up of lives.' Luttwak, *Turbo-Capitalism*, p. xi.

48. N. Luhmann, *Trust and Power* (Eng. tr. Chichester, 1979).

49. On the destandardisation of the working career see Beck, *Risk Society*, pp. 139–49.

50. For an eloquent account of the moral effects of the casualisation of labour see R. Sennett, *The Corrosion of Character* (New York and London, 1999).

51. See W. Benjamin, 'The storyteller', in *Illuminations* (Eng. tr. London, 1970), pp. 83–109.

52. H. Pieron, *L'évolution de la mémoire* (Paris, 1910), p. 353.

53. E. L. Eisenstein, 'Some conjectures about the impact of printing on western society and thought: a preliminary report', *Journal of Modern History*, 40:1 (1968), pp. 1–56.

54. Benjamin, *Gesammelte Schriften*, vol. v, p. 717. On the limited speed of the transmission of news in the nineteenth century see G. Storey, *Reuter's Century, 1851–1951* (London, 1951).

55. J. Romein, *The Watershed of Two Eras: Europe in 1900* (New York, 1976), pp. 264–6.

56. B. Anderson, *Imagined Communities* (London, 1991), pp. 22–36.

57. Benjamin, 'The storyteller', pp. 83–109.

58. M. Castells, *The Rise of the Network Society* (Oxford, 1996), pp. 328, 329, 330–4, 339–40, 367, 371.

59. Ibid., pp. 336–7.

60. M. K. Matsuda, *The Memory of the Modern* (New York and Oxford, 1996), p. 171.

61. Kennedy, *Preparing for the Twenty-First Century*, p. 52.

62. Ibid., p. 52.

63. Ibid., p. 52.

64. T. Kidder, *The Soul of a New Machine* (New York, 1981), p. 137.

65. Pieron, *L'Évolution de la mémoire*, p. 353.

66. Nowotny, *Time*, p. 39.

67. S. Turkle, *Life on the Screen: Identity in the Age of the Internet* (New York, 1995).

68. R. Barglow, *The Crisis of the Self in the Age of Information* (London, 1994).

69. W. Benjamin, *Charles Baudelaire: A Lyric Poet in the Era of High Capitalism* (Eng. tr. London and New York, 1973), p. 51.

70. Attali, *Noise*, p. 123.

71. Ibid., p. 27.

72. Benjamin, *Charles Baudelaire*, p. 131.

73. Brain, *Going to the Fair*.

74. M. Proust, *Remembrance of Things Past* (tr. C. K. Scott Moncrieff and T. Kilmartin, Harmondsworth, 1983), vol. i, pp. 47–8.

75. J. Crary, 'Spectacle, attention, counter-memory', *October*, 50 (1989), pp. 97–107.

76. J-L. Comolli, 'Machines of the visible', in T. de Laurentis and S. Heath, eds., *The Cinematic Apparatus* (New York, 1980).

4   Topographies of forgetting

If, then, the spatial frameworks of a culture, the way in which we set about the task of producing spaces, occupies a pivotal role in the localisation of cultural memory, if it establishes a *topography of remembering*, then this might lead us on to ask the further question and to return us to the question posed at an earlier stage: what is the effect of the produced spaces of *contemporary culture* on the transmission of cultural memory?

Its effect, I want to suggest, is to generate a particular kind of *cultural amnesia*; and, for the sake of heuristic convenience, I should like to distinguish three features of contemporary human settlement, which are inextricably intertwined, the investigation of which will help us to understand how this condition of cultural forgetting is generated. The first is the scale of human settlement. The second is the production of speed. The third is the repeated intentional destruction of the built environment. These phenomena are to be explained, in their turn, by the particular moment we have now reached in the capitalist process of production.

I

The 'art of memory' was a European rhetorical tradition which was sustained for some fifteen hundred years, from, let us say, Cicero to Leibniz. Ideas are not contextless; and in understanding this tradition of thinking about place memory, this 'method of loci' as its practitioners styled it, we need to keep in mind the characteristic life-spaces, what might be called the scale of emplacement, within which these conventions of rhetoric flourished. As the practice of an intellectual elite, this would have been a city world; but if we were able to walk through these cities we would immediately be struck by the concentration of people in a geographic space that by modern standards would appear minuscule. These were urban entities which came into existence behind well-equipped fortress walls and where the city ground plans took their shape and meaning from the distinctive opposition between city and land, between centre and periphery. What distinguished towns in the Middle Ages from the villages, estates and manorial settlements that covered much of the European plain was that these towns and cities closed themselves off from the rural environment in order to enlarge the scope and intensity of their communication with the wider world. These urban entities were a crossroads within a wall.[1]

The first thing we need to notice, then, is the small scale of early modern European settlements. In 1400 the most common type of European town was the local marketing centre. These tiny places, many little different from farming villages, which had fewer than 2,000 residents, constituted the overwhelming majority of all urban settlements and housed over half the urban population of Europe.[2] In 1400 only four European cities – Paris, Milan, Bruges and Venice – had populations of more than 100,000 inhabitants, while the tenth largest city in Europe, Ghent, had a population of 70,000 inhabitants.[3] In 1500 London had a population of 50,000 and even two centuries later the next largest English city after London numbered only 20,000. In general, territorial groups organised medieval communes. Venice was informally organised into neighbourhoods, each with its own church, square, quay and well, defining a territory within which much of the daily life of the residents took place; and Genoa's political, military and judicial structures were territorially ordered around eight *compagne*. The citizens of medieval communes had a daily familiarity with a large part of their environment; in all but the few largest cities, the whole of the urban space was easily accessible on foot. Shown a square mile of Venice on a map after looking at a square mile on the map of any of ten or fifteen present-day major North American and European cities, an observer is likely to ask if the map of Venice is truly drawn at the same scale as the others.

The spatial memorability of early modern European settlements, grounded in their small scale, was definitively reinforced
by two further features of pre-eminent importance: their perimeter,
and their point of central focus. One of the most distinctive elements of town design was its perimeter.[4] To this general rule there
were, indeed, exceptions; in a few parts of Europe, particularly in
many English market towns and in some settlements in the Spanish
Netherlands, there remained a substantial number of unwalled
towns. But most cities provided themselves with a clearly demarcated
perimeter, an easily recognisable outline formed by fortifications,
gates and towers, and many had heavy stone walls, built particularly during the period between 1100 and 1500. Not that such walls
formed permanent barriers; as towns grew, they incorporated the surrounding land and population by building new fortifications; Paris
constructed five such lines of walls between 1180 and 1845. Then, at
the centre of these towns, Gothic cathedrals were of such magnitude
as to dominate the entire urban landscape; by providing an orientation towards one building, they endowed the city as a whole with a
monolithic character. In every city where a cathedral was erected
from the late twelfth century onwards, it was the largest building
ever built there and it would remain so until the twentieth century.
This was so of the cathedrals of Florence and Milan in fifteenth- and
sixteenth-century Italy; it was so with the cathedrals of the imperial
cities of Central Europe such as Ulm and Nordlingen; and in many
French towns – Lyon, Chartres, Amiens, Bourges – the cathedral provided the focal point around which the layout of streets and markets
was organised. All these cathedrals were disproportionate in size to
the city they dominated; their existence effectively eliminated the
very possibility of any competing undertaking. Enclosed within their
clearly demarcated perimeter, this orientation of the city towards
one single building created an effect of spatial cohesion, and hence
of memorability, which remained in force whether the cathedral was
viewed from a distance or whether it was viewed from close up, and
the sense of cohesion persisted from every vantage point.[5]

The period from 1500 to 1750, it is true, was marked by concentrated urban growth, with large-scale new baroque capitals and
mercantile centres concentrating royal authority and the organisation of national and overseas commerce. By the late sixteenth century, London, Amsterdam, Paris, Madrid, Lisbon and half a dozen
other cities all had a population of at least 100,000 and in some
instances as much as 250,000. Whereas in the mid sixteenth century
Paris and London, the largest cities north of the Alps, had 130,000
and 60,000 inhabitants respectively, they were approaching the half
million mark by 1650. The growth of Madrid is particularly striking
testimony to the impact of absolutist monarchies in creating a new
urbanisation based on government employment: a town with only a
few thousand inhabitants in 1561, it grew to 65,000 by 1600 and to
170,000 by 1630.[6] By the mid eighteenth century a new urban hierarchy had come into being in Europe. Where there were only four
cities with more than 100,000 inhabitants in 1500, twenty-four had
reached this total by the beginning of the nineteenth century. From
a medieval peak of some 200,000 inhabitants, the summits of the
urban hierarchy grew to 500,000 by 1700 and to more than a million
by 1800. In the period from 1300 to 1800 overall, Europe experienced
something never before seen outside the Mediterranean basin: the
growth of very large urban entities.[7]

Yet, as Girouard has observed, it was still possible two hundred years ago to see the whole of any city in the world.[8] You could
see London from Highgate, Paris from Montmartre, Rome from
Monte Mario. An astonishing amount of Venice could be found in
one square mile; most of the Grand Canal, and everything from near
the railway station in the north-west to the Arsenal in the east, is in
that area. One square mile of Rome could include the Piazza Venezia,
the Via del Corso, the Piazza Navona, the Pantheon and the Trevi
Fountain. Almost all of central Amsterdam, including its major canal
system, fits into such an area. Two hundred years ago it still made
sense to speak metaphorically of a bird's eye view of a city. Those
who wanted to portray the city would climb to the top of a cathedral,

belfry, or central tower in order to grasp visually from a single point of view the entire urban space they intended to describe.[9] Eighteenth-century vistas of Venice indicate that the domes of Salute, Redentore, St Mark's, and San Giorgio Maggiore all need to be viewed as a unit.[10] Eighteenth-century engravings of Vienna, such as the monumental engraving by Joseph Daniel Hopfer commissioned by Empress Maria Theresa in 1769, represent the city as a closed entity.[11] There still exists a bird's eye view of Amsterdam in 1544, after an engraving by Cornelis Anthoniszoon.[12] Most cities, indeed, had an easily recognisable outline, a perimeter of fortifications, gates and towers. Laid out before your eyes, if you climbed to a high spot in any city, was a kind of urban forest of roofs, towers, domes and spires, but you could still see that the forest had edges and a circumference. The circuit of walls girdling the medieval city might have gone, and the size of the city may have grown, but the human eye could still survey the city as a whole and be convinced that it had a perceptible gestalt. The inhabitants lived with and could envisage the view of a *bounded* city.

The mark of modernity is the dismantling of the city frontier, the effacement of the self-evident and uncontested city form for which the gestalt of the fortified city had provided the model. No longer seen as a fixed and delimited form, the city becomes a labile and mobile whole that, in principle, develops endlessly. The nineteenth-century city becomes formless.[13] Mining centres, mills, metallurgical complexes spring up in a growth that is rapid, unplanned and largely unregulated. Aside from calculations regarding the logistics of transporting bulky products, these new life-spaces have little form; and as they spread they merge into an entirely new type of urban concentration. How is this formlessness to be named? Some areas are called the Black Country or the Five Towns. Some are named after a natural feature which their growth so quickly smothers, like the Ruhr Valley. Some are named after the work done there, like the Borinage, which means coal extraction. The generic term which best fits these dense yet weakly centralised regions is the one coined by Patrick Geddes to denote any very large urban area: the conurbation.

In the great cities of the late nineteenth century – London, Paris, Berlin, New York – even if you climbed a hill you could no longer see the whole of the city; the edges of the urban forest could not be surveyed any more. If you wanted to see the whole of a city you now had to go several thousand feet up in an aeroplane. It is difficult to overstate the magnitude of the mutation in urban history brought about by the emergence of the giant city. There was no city of a million inhabitants in the west from the end of the Roman Empire until the eighteenth century, when London attained that figure, and no city of half that size, with the exception of Paris and Naples. But in 1900 Europe contained nine cities of over a million inhabitants – London, Paris, Berlin, Vienna, St Petersburg, Manchester, Birmingham, Moscow and Glasgow – and a further twenty-two between a half a million and a million.[14] Because of the new constitution of the urban proletariat, uncertain from one day to the next about lodging and employment, the city paves the way for a great uprooting, the remarkable *massive rupture* between persons and places.

The massive change in the scale of cities was due above all to the physical separation between the place of residence and the place of work. The transformation from a tight integration of work and residence to a spatial organisation in which workplaces and residences were disposed in different clusters was the central feature in the large-scale industrialisation of nineteenth-century England.[15] It has been closely documented for Leicester,[16] for Birmingham,[17] for Coventry[18] and for Leeds;[19] even in London, where craft production survived as the dominant form throughout the nineteenth century, there was a sorting out into single-purpose, specialised neighbourhoods and a large-scale separation of work spaces and living spaces.[20] The emergence of this new type of human settlement occurred in distinctively different ways in different types of cities. Some, like Chicago and Pittsburgh, were started anew; some, like Lille and Essen, were built on the foundations of older villages or smaller cities; some, like the suburban extensions of Paris and London, grew on the outskirts of existing major cities. Yet even such different cases as are to be found on the continents of Europe and America demonstrate the same fundamental principle at work. Even though the new European urbanisation was modified by the more historically layered character of continental cities, the impact of industrialisation was decisively registered by the taking down of city walls in mid-nineteenth-century Paris, Vienna, Brussels, Geneva, Madrid and Stockholm.[21] The most extreme instance of the change in scale was in the New World. Just as Americans saw the natural world around them as limitless, so they envisaged the spaces of human settlement as subject to no natural limitation but as capable of infinite expansion; the grid system, extending block after block, was in principle boundless.[22]

Yet – and it is an extremely important qualification – the lived space of the new industrial working classes was still structured on what was, by modern standards, a small scale.[23] Though dwelling place and working place were separated, they were not distant. The factory town of the mid nineteenth century remained a community where people walked to and from work, and this continued to be the case until the introduction of tramways and bicycles at the end of the century.[24] Mining settlements were more like villages than towns. The major cotton-mill towns of Britain in 1870, then at their industrial peak, contained between 30,000 and 80,000 inhabitants. Clydebank, with its major shipyards, chemical works and distilleries, had 22,000 inhabitants in 1901. In England, the organisation of industrial disputes by trade union branches often took place in pubs, where landlords acted as strike coordinators or union treasurers, and Friendly Societies, the main self-help community organisation for workers, also gathered in ale houses.[25] In France, under the Second Republic and Second Empire, workers were able to develop a militant class consciousness in relatively free social spaces, informal working-class gathering places such as cafés, taverns, cabarets, dance halls and theatres.[26] In Europe generally, the real strength of the big city labour movements resided in what were in effect urban villages, townships within cities: Floridsdorf in Vienna, Wedding in Berlin, Sans in

Barcelona, Sesto San Giovanni in Milan. Anyone who doubts that we are still talking about communities in the strong sense of the term, where the feeling for a particular place remained crucial and enduring, should recall the early history of football clubs. Of the sixteen leading teams in the First Division of the English Football League in the early 1890s, eleven came from towns ranging from 60,000 to 200,000, while the three which came from parts of giant cities (Manchester, Liverpool and Birmingham) were named not after the city but after the neighbourhood or borough within it (Newton Heath, Everton and Aston), a practice repeated when the subsequently founded London football teams were named after neighbourhoods – Chelsea, Crystal Palace, Charlton, Leyton, Tottenham and West Ham.

To bring these facts into relief is to remind ourselves of how radically different these life-spaces were from the emerging spatial order that characterises the most materially advanced forms of contemporary civilisation. What is now developing is a new form of settlement space. Just as Engels in the 1840s located the most advanced spatial example of the new industrial capitalism in Manchester, so now Gottdiener sees today's equivalent in the dispersed spatial arrangements of the United States in the 1980s.[27] He summarises the difference in the contrast between the 'bounded city form' and what he calls the 'polynucleated metropolitan region'. By this he means to emphasise the fact that the currently emerging spatial order is best understood not as a larger version of the city, even the giant city, but as possessing certain new structural peculiarities of its own. These new features make the old model of urban development increasingly inaccurate in describing contemporary spatial phenomena. In the past, the study of urban life was focussed on a particular image of urban spatial structure, the bounded city form, where capital, production, people and power were concentrated in the city centre, and where correspondingly it seemed appropriate to have an image of spatial integration as forming a series of concentric zones. What we now increasingly have are metropolitan populations distributed in ever expanding regional areas that are not only massive in scope but amorphous in form. Polynucleated growth is characterised above all by this process of deconcentration: the massive regional dispersal of people, commerce, industry and administration along with the contemporary restructuring of such regions into multicentred realms – sprawling for miles and miles and located everywhere in the country, especially in those areas once thought immune from urban development.[28]

These life-spaces form the emerging spatial order that characterises the most materially advanced forms of contemporary civilisation. Whereas in 1900 only one-tenth of the world's population lived in cities, a century later half the population lives in cities. While Europe in 1900 contained nine cities with over a million inhabitants, by 1990 there were thirty-five cities in the world with populations of over 5 million, twenty-two of them in the developing world; and by 2000 it was estimated that there would be fifty-seven cities over the 5 million mark, forty-four in the developing world.[29] By 1992 there were already thirteen megacities – Tokyo, São Paolo, New York, Ciudad de Mexico, Shanghai, Bombay, Los Angeles, Buenos Aires, Seoul, Beijing, Rio de Janeiro, Calcutta, Osaka – which, as nodes of the global economy, constituted very large agglomerations of over 10 million.[30]

What may become the most representative urban reconfiguration of the twenty-first century is the Southern China metropolis, an emerging megacity connecting Hong Kong, Shenzhen, Guangzhou, Zhuhai and Macau, in a spatial structure extending over 50,000 square kilometres and embracing a population of between 40 and 50 million, depending upon where you define the boundaries. In the mid 1990s this space still had no name. Yet, although its component parts are still spatially discontinuously dispersed throughout a predominantly rural landscape, it is a spatial system bound together by a backbone of internal linkages, with a net of railways, freeways, hovercraft, boats and planes, with five new airports being built in Hong Kong, Macau, Shenzhen, Zhuhai and Guangzhou, and with nearby container ports under construction in Hong Kong, Shenzhen,

Zhuhai, Guangzhou and Macau. Though it is nameless it is rapidly becoming an interdependent unit.[31]

The history of the city in the twentieth century has been a story of dispersal. As the story of the radiocentric city nears its end we become suspicious of centring devices and we refer so readily to the decentred subject because the subject's current characteristic mode of emplacement takes place in life-spaces which are themselves decentred. So when Lynch, in *The Image of the City* of 1960,[32] described the metropolis as a place of well-defined nodes, pathways, edges, landmarks and districts, he was being nostalgic; whereas Frank Lloyd Wright was being prescient in 1932 when he wrote that 'the future city will be everywhere and nowhere, and it will be a city so greatly different from the ancient city or any city of today that we will probably fail to recognize its coming as the city at all'.[33] In life-spaces so changed in their scale of emplacement that the city becomes less and less a physical entity that might yield a point of focus, one of the fundamental preconditions, which the art of memory as a method of loci took for granted as something which goes without saying, is blurred beyond recognition.

2

This preliminary view of the scale of human settlement leads us naturally to consider the second of the processes which I isolated earlier: *the production of speed.*[34]

The supersession of walking by mechanised modes of movement in the nineteenth century was signalled by the metaphor of circulation, with its triple allusion to the movement of traffic, the circulation of goods and the circulation of the blood; and many of the invented rituals of the century were rituals of speed, every triumph over the tyranny of distance, from the inauguration of rail links to the opening of the Suez Canal, providing the occasion for elaborate celebrations. By the end of the century the capitalist world's reconfiguration on the basis of modern traffic, though not complete, was already evident. Machines of mobility – trains, steamships, bicycles, elevators, escalators, automobiles, aeroplanes – transformed the relationship between sight and bodily movement.[35] The look was being mobilised by mechanical rides.[36] The Eiffel Tower of 1889 featured an elevator ascending at over 2 metres per second; the Chicago Exhibition of 1893 displayed a Ferris Wheel and a mechanical ride through a movement machine; at the first public projection of films in 1895 the audience witnessed the arrival of a train at a station in the Lumière brothers' *L'arrivée du train en gare*; at the Paris Exhibition of 1900, 3.5 kilometres of moving track, a *trottoir roulant* or moving pavement with three speeds, transported spectators through the exhibition space as if they were goods on a conveyer belt; and in the Russian exhibit, visitors could board 21-metre-long railway carriages, fully equipped with dining rooms, smoking rooms and bedrooms, to take part in a 'virtual trip' on the Trans-Siberian Railway, a virtual tour which condensed the fourteen-day trip from Moscow to Peking into 45 minutes.

We witness here the emergence of a new mode of perception – a panoramic perception – which precipitates a new relationship between the perceiver and the object-world, where the perceiver, instead of belonging to the same space as the perceived objects, sees those objects through the mechanical apparatus which moves the perceiver through the world; here the motion produced by the machine is integral to the act of visual perception itself in the sense that the perceiver can only see things in mechanised motion. If the railway journey yielded the prototype of panoramic perception, its most typical modern instance is the motorway; envisioned as a spatial conductor for conveying traffic in a frictionless flow, the highway has become perhaps the most romanticised structure of the twentieth-century built environment. In his 1986 film *Reichsautobahn*, Bitomsky accomplishes something like an archaeology of past perception by re-presenting the autobahn at the moment of its first imagining; decomposing original cinema footage into its individual images, by close analysis of single film scenes, by slowing down film shots, and by scrutinising frame enlargements, he conclusively demonstrates the representational work of early cinema in the intoxicating speed of the autobahns which became the most massively filmed construction project of the century.[37] Seen through the windshield of an automobile, the German landscape, as Dimendberg has well shown, transformed by the carefully positioned twists and turns of the new highways into a manufactured pastoral, reminded many observers at the time of a scene from an aeroplane;[38] just as the American variant of the technological sublime, exhibited at the 1939 World's Fair, featured film footage of cars travelling on the model highway of the Futurama, where the sweep of the camera over the landscape anticipated the view of a typical suburban setting as one might witness it today from the window of an aeroplane.[39]

Motorways now appear so natural that we have to make an effort to imagine a world without them; but when they were being built they were so unfamiliar that an effort was required to imagine oneself into them. But the German and the American intoxication with freeways reveals the motorway as not solely a solution to a traffic problem but a feature of the social imaginary, not just a piece of material practice but a labour of representation. The autobahn bridges and the lane dividers in the traffic scheme of Bel Geddes were far more than elaborate pieces of engineering; they were metaphors in which the flow of vehicles represented fantasies of national unity and unimpeded circulation. Indeed, by mid-century the degree of collective libido invested in highways had reached the point where the modern automobile and its motorways were spoken of quite explicitly as being as integral to our lives as were the forum and the acropolis to the lives of the ancients. Motorways, it has been said, are the pyramids of the twentieth century.[40]

The comparison made here is not simply a conceit or hyperbole, in the sense that it registers adequately a fundamental structural change of spatial values: that is to say, a shift in the relationship between the two main components of all cultural landscapes or topographies – settlements, and pathways connecting settlements. The outstanding feature of the modern cultural landscape, increasingly, is the dominance of pathways over settlements.[41]

Traffic engineering tends to supersede town planning; and this mass production of speed has been gradually effacing the distinction between dwelling and travelling. We no longer live in societies dominated by relatively stationary zones but rather by ones characterised by their nodes of passage. Well over half a century ago Musil may have thought he caricatured when, in *The Man Without Qualities*, he depicted 'a kind of super-American city where everyone rushes about, or stands still, with a stop-watch in his hand,... Overhead trains, overground trains, underground trains, pneumatic express mails carrying consignments of human beings, chains of motor vehicles all racing along horizontally, express lifts vertically pumping crowds from one traffic level to another';[42] and later Gertrude Stein thought it was 'something strictly American to conceive of space that is filled always filled with moving';[43] but the steady uninterrupted flow of traffic which she thought of as a universal American requirement is now widely diffused.

The universal diffusion of traffic began to take firm hold over the human habitat following the Second World War; it was at that point that a series of industries, focussed on a number of regions in the world economy – the Midwest of the United States, the West Midlands in Great Britain, the Ruhr-Rhineland and the Tokyo-Yokohama region – concentrated on the manufacture of cars, ships, planes and transport equipment. In the immediate post-war period these were among the major propellants of economic growth. In its train have come a proliferation of transit points: airports, hotel chains, large retail outlets. Bofill and Castells are in agreement that the new architectural monuments of our epoch are likely to be built as 'communication exchanges' – train stations, airports, harbours, telecommunication infrastructures, computerised trading centres.[44]

This mass production of speed has been gradually effacing the distinction between dwelling and travelling. We need to think a little more closely about what the effacement of the distinction between dwelling and travelling implies. Contemporary Paris, to take a single instance, is a topography of more or less *continuous displacement*.[45] In 1972 there were 7 million daily displacements inside Paris and over 12 million daily displacements in the Paris region. Some 850,000 people commuted daily from Paris to the suburbs; 200,000 went daily from Paris to jobs outside; 900,000 suburbanites travelled daily to employment in the suburbs; 700,000 inhabitants of Paris travelled daily to employment within the city. The Parisian or the suburbanite spent on average two hours a day in transport, the equivalent of one quarter of working time. During a single hour when the greatest concentration of movement took place, more than 700,000 people were found to be using public transport, with 300,000 in the Métro and 230,000 passing though the railway stations. The figures may be taken as emblematic. Every day there are over 100,000 people in the air.[46] At Dallas Fort Worth they serve 30 million passengers a year. The airport has become a new kind of crossroads, a kind of miniature city that abstracts from the historical and cultural specificity, the temporal layering, of all previous cities. We increasingly occupy a *space of flows* rather than a *space of places*.[47]

Topography is read through the car. We use a car not to see a city but to gain freedom of movement; but the view from the car's windows is often our primary experience of urban space, and much everyday knowledge of our life-spaces is learned through a windshield. So Rayner Banham can write that 'Like earlier generations of English intellectuals who taught themselves Italian in order to read Dante in the original, I learned to drive in order to read Los Angeles in the original.'[48] The driver of a motor vehicle has the perception of a kind of abstract subject equipped with the capacity to read the symbols of the highway code, concerned only with steering to the destination, looking about to see only what needs to be seen for that purpose; the route is seen solely from the angle of its functionality. Space thus appears in a reduced form: volume yields to surface, any overall view surrenders to visual signals spaced out along fixed trajectories already mapped out in the plan. Speed, as it were, cancels out the ground and territorial reference points, and driving achieves what Virilio calls 'the aesthetics of disappearance'. This is why Baudrillard calls speed 'the triumph of instantaneity over time as depth', the 'triumph of forgetting over memory' and, with characteristic hyperbole, 'a spectacular form of amnesia'. The rule of speed, he says, is to leave no trace behind. In *The View From the Road*, Appleyard, Lynch and Myer describe the driving experience as 'a sequence played to the eyes of a captive, somewhat fearful, but particularly attentive audience, whose vision is filtered and directed forward'.[49] In this driving space, where the post-urban civilisation represented by Los Angeles is being born, a metropolis of seventy-six different cities where alleyways are ten-lane freeways and where, as Umberto Eco has so elegantly put it in his *Travels in Hyperreality*, man considers his left foot an atrophied appendix, because cars no longer have a clutch, eyes are something to focus, at steady driving speed, on visual-mechanical wonders, on signs, constructions that must impress the mind in the space of a few seconds.[50]

Cars restructure topography by destroying the street as a place for gathering. Since the level of social interaction between neighbours in a given street is inversely related to the amount of traffic passing through it, cars undermine the cohesive social structures of the city by eroding shared social space. They require space to have essentially the function of permitting motion so that this space becomes meaningless unless it can be subordinated to free movement. The overall effect is to divide the urban fabric into two types of space. The first type is urban space which fulfils a single function. To this category belong the business district, the industrial zone, the residential suburb, the housing estate, the shopping mall, the car park, the ring-road, the underpass and the sealed machine of the car itself. The second type is urban space which Michael Walzer has called 'open-minded'. To this category belong the bustling square, the market, the lively street, the pavement café and the park. In the first type of space we are in a hurry; in the second type of space we are more ready to acknowledge the existence of other people, and might even go so far as to exchange friendly words with them. The reconfiguration of urban topography by the car means that the second type of space is steadily and inexorably eclipsed by the first.[51]

The great initiator of this new type of topography, it is true, predates the car: it was Haussmann who taught subsequent urban planners to subordinate all functions of urban settlement to the road as a carrier of vehicular traffic and to disregard the movement of pedestrians; his network of arterial connections constituted what he described as a 'general circulatory system', subdivided into tributary systems, each organised around a plaza, which in turn is no longer a place in itself but a traffic node, what Haussmann called a 'node of relation'. It was the subsequent diffusion of cars that made this topographical reconfiguring prototypical. The anticipation of increasingly high levels of car use – with car ownership more than doubling in Europe between 1970 and 1995, and with an estimated 500 million cars in the world today – has led planners to design cities around traffic specifications, treating people who move by their own locomotion and on unscheduled paths as of little interest, thus effectively encouraging ever-increasing car use.[52] London's grand spaces, like Parliament Square, Piccadilly Circus, Trafalgar Square, Hyde Park Corner and Marble Arch, are all now overwhelmed by cars; and shopping mall planners, Haussmann's heirs, employ a mechanist rhetoric he would have well understood when they speak of magnet stores, of generators, of flow and of pull.

What is lost, with this, is the idea of a city in which one can, as it were, 'read' buildings at a pedestrian's pace. A whole network of previous pedestrian expectations are thereby lost. The words we used to describe the street reveal something of the expectations that were formerly brought to it. We find a whole set of words – path, track, parade, promenade, mall – all of which are connected with ways of proceeding on foot. All of these words indicate that pedestrian movement along a set way, the delimitation of the way as an extended public space, is deeply embedded in human experience. From its inception, the road was freighted with metaphoric meaning;[53] everyone knows that the path to salvation is straight, that if a criminal is to reform his ways he must try to go straight, and that the road to hell is paved with good intentions. Hegel, expressing his admiration of the French revolutionaries, wrote to a friend in January 1807 of the *ancien régime* institutions as being like 'those children's shoes, become too tight, that hinder the gait, and that the revolutionaries soon get rid of'. This was more than a figure of speech; it echoed Roman law which had already long ago decreed that 'where the feet are, there is the fatherland'.[54] Engels was aware of the same phenomenon; in June 1848 he remarked that 'the first assemblies take place on the large boulevards, where Parisian life circulates with the greatest intensity'.[55] He was right; for the proletarian masses from the country and the suburbs, the simple fact of penetrating to the heart of Paris, in 1848 and in 1871, of feeling under their feet its avenues and its opulent streets, was a tangible appropriation, a concrete way of diminishing a real and measurable social and political distance between the masses and the concentrated power of the bourgeois state. Goebbels, after his fashion, could not but agree; in 1931, during the National Socialists' struggle against the Marxist parties in Berlin, he declared that 'whoever can conquer the streets also conquers the state'.[56]

So that when Barthes says that 'we speak our city ... simply by living in it, by travelling through it, by looking at it',[57] we can go on to elaborate that thought by saying that the idea of speaking our city is not simply a conceit; for, as Michel de Certeau suggests, the act of walking is to the urban system what the act of speaking is to the language system. The pedestrian act – in analogy with the speech act – may be said, then, to have a threefold 'uttering' function: it is a process of appropriation of the topographic system by the pedestrian (just as the speaker appropriates language); it is a spatial realisation of the site (just as the act of speaking is a sonic realisation of language); and it implies relationships among distant positions, that is to say pragmatic 'contracts' in the form of movements (just as verbal utterance is 'allocution' and sets up 'contracts' between fellow speakers).[58] There are quite specific ways, then, in which walking may be described as a space of utterance; as speech is to language, so walking is to the appropriation of urban space.

To speak of walking in such a way is at once to illuminate and to etherealise its implications for us. For its effect is more fundamental than that. Walking – and we are not speaking here analogically – is a quintessentially *integrative* activity. That this is the case is indicated by forms of expression by means of which we refer to deficient processes of walking, as, for instance, when we speak of someone being impeded, or walking disjointedly, or limping, or tottering, all of which terms signal the absence of the integrative force the necessary quality of which is otherwise found to be present and efficacious in the act of walking. Walking demonstrates to me that I am what Husserl calls a 'total organism'[59] articulated into a number of particular organs, that in walking I am able to constitute myself as a coherent organism; the unity of my body parts is precipitated by the kinaesthetic feelings associated with the actual movements of my body as I walk. Every time I engage in the activity of walking I am building up a coherent world, a world which contains both the near-sphere of familiar and accessible experiences and the far-sphere of unfamiliar and unknown things; I bring together both spheres in a unified 'ensemble'. Moreover, if my lived space is present to me in the form of what Husserl calls a 'fixed system of places', that is because walking establishes 'oriented things' as identical things and hence constitutes a 'steady system of places'.[60] Walking is at once an act of organic self-unification, and an act which builds up for me a coherent environment. Whereas for Lacan the 'mirror stage' generates an *illusory* sense of the unity of the subject, for Husserl the activity of walking precipitates an *authentic* integration of the subject.

If our spatial memory is to work effectively a certain measure of stability is required; the rhetorical art of memory is insistent upon, and could not have existed without reference to, a stable system of places. This stability of our place system is eroded by the production of speed, because machines which produce mobility – trains, automobiles, planes, bicycles, elevators, escalators, moving walkways – undermine the assumption that what is visible is also stable. Machines of mobility endow what is seen with a quality of evanescence. Early accounts of railway travel highlight the difficulty of recognising anything in the landscape traversed beyond its broadest outlines; Burckhardt observed that on a train journey 'it is no longer possible to really distinguish the objects closest to one – trees, shacks, and such: as soon as one turns to take a look at them they already are long gone'.[61] This new experience of evanescence, initially produced by the railway and later celebrated in Impressionism and Futurism, is now ubiquitous and incessant; today's fast-moving transport constantly mobilises our field of vision. The fleeting sight of giant billboards, the momentary view of a street scene, a peripheral view glimpsed through the window of a train – these have long become naturalised as everyday occurrences, and habitualised over again through our perception of film. Film – which gives us, in Godard's words, truth twenty-four times a second – is the visual art form that most effectively articulates this reconfigured perception; developing alongside one another, the medium of film and the topography of the city problematise the assumption that the visible is the stable.

3

The effects of the production of speed are reinforced by a third feature of contemporary human settlement: *the repeated intentional destruction of the built environment.* When Engels wrote *The Condition of the Working Class in England in 1844,* he found that workers' housing, which was built by speculators for fast profits, was constructed to last for only forty years. According to a survey conducted in 1936, most buildings in London other than the relatively few recognised 'historic' ones were, on average, renewed in thirty years and abandoned in sixty; the rate of replacement in the central sections of American cities is faster.[62] Long ago, returning to

New York after many years of absence, Henry James saw an urban landscape possessed by 'the reiterated sacrifice to pecuniary profit' and 'in perpetual repudiation of the past'; 'we are only installments, symbols, stop-gaps', the proud villas seem to say, 'we have nothing to do with continuity, responsibility, transmission'.[63] Throughout his American journey Tocqueville was struck by what seemed to him to be the impermanence and insubstantial character of American settlement; houses seemed to be stage sets rather than buildings meant to last, and the city was treated by its citizens simply as a complicated installation of offices and restaurants and shops for the conduct of business.[64] Buckminster Fuller was making essentially the same point when he described New York as a 'continual evolutionary process of evacuations, demolitions, removals, temporarily vacant lots, new installations'.[65]

At the beginning of the 1930s Siegfried Kracauer devoted considerable reflection to the transience of urban topography. He found in Berlin its unparalleled exemplar; and he took Paris as his point of contrast. A German from Berlin who comes to Paris, he wrote, 'believes he has been transplanted into a huge provincial town' because 'life and society seem to him to be those of a hundred years ago';[66] for Paris 'carries the signs of age upon its brow. Out of the pores of its houses there spring up memories.'[67] Paris, like Berlin, has 'endless streets', but no Parisian streets compare with what he calls the 'unhistorical nature' of Berlin's streets. The Kurfürstendamm of the early 1930s, for example, embodies a kind of empty flowing time in which nothing is allowed to last.[68] The 'rootlessness' of its ever-changing shops 'effaces the memory' of what they have replaced. On the Kurfürstendamm what has passed away 'makes its exit without leaving behind any traces'; 'the new enterprises are always absolutely new and those that have been displaced by them are totally extinguished'. 'When one Berlin shop is replaced by another', let us say a tearoom by a confectioner's shop, the former's reality 'is not merely superseded but so completely displaced as if it never existed at all. Through its complete presentness it is plunged into a state of being forgotten from which no force can ever any longer rescue it.'[69] Many of Berlin's buildings had been stripped of their ornaments which formed a kind of bridge to yesterday; only the marble staircases that glimmer through the doorway preserve memories, those of the pre-war world first class. In other cities, too, images of squares, company names and enterprises are transformed; 'but only in Berlin are the transformations of the past so radically stripped from memory'.[70] Berlin is quintessentially 'the place in which one quickly forgets; indeed, it appears as if this city has control of the magical means of eradicating all memories'.[71]

This process of creative destruction was propelled by the invention of new building materials, making for lightness, openness and speed. The world of the late nineteenth century was obsessed by what was coming to be felt increasingly as the burden of the past. It did not yet know the unbearable lightness of being. Its urban fabric was a world of painstakingly finished ornamentation, carefully chipped and smoothed surfaces, cobbles, stairs, ponderous piers, immovable monuments. The urban fabric of the early twentieth century was one of high-tensile steels, steel-reinforced concrete, high-strength glass, walls reduced to reflective skins, highways, escalators, demountable exhibitions.

This process can be perceived to be the pattern of construction under capitalism. Both our urban hierarchies and our transport systems demonstrate the acceleration in the pace at which our produced landscapes are transformed.[72] Capitalism continually restructures our urban landscapes through suburbanisation, deindustrialisation, gentrification and urban renewal. And capitalism annihilates space through its fixed investment in rail, road and port systems, because at some point the impulsion to continue to annihilate space must make these initial investments obsolete and redundant. Marx already recognised the principle at work.[73] The more production comes to rest on exchange, he wrote, the more important do the physical conditions of exchange – the means of communication and transport – become for the costs of circulation; while capital must on the one side strive to tear down every spatial barrier and conquer the whole world for its market, it strives on the other side to annihilate this space with time. So whether we look at our urban hierarchies or at our transportation systems we see the same process at work: there is a perpetual struggle in which physical landscapes appropriate to capitalism's requirements are produced at a particular historical moment only to be destroyed or disrupted at a subsequent historical moment.

Cultural memory is eroded in this process because the *building blocks* of the city have been broken down.[74] The district, the square, and the street were the basic building blocks of the city, and it is their breakdown which generates a diffuse cultural amnesia. The district: because the dense district, a more or less well-defined cluster or group, has been replaced by a scattered distribution of slab-like buildings which can only be recognised or imagined as a totality or gestalt from an aeroplane. The square: because the square, an enclosure, what Lynch called a 'distinct and unforgettable place', has been modified in its overall effect on the city gestalt by the parking lot. And the street: because the modern street has become merely a means of communication in a grid system which is, to be sure, orderly and in that sense easy to describe, but is nonetheless altogether unmemorable; with respect to the United States, even if not to Europe, we may ask ourselves: was that 92nd Street or 93rd Street? When urban structures are no longer in this way clearly defined in terms of districts, squares and streets, our public environment comes to be made up out of spaces that are not so much localised places as rather spaces that diffuse and erode the public realm.

The breaking down of these building blocks, the district, the square and the street, is not simply a direct attack on the body of the city; it is an indirect attack on the human body too.[75] For man is, as Marcel Mauss said, the rhythmic animal, socially and individually; and the human body, for its rhythmic action, requires privileged points in space and time: that is to say, central and high places as well as borders and thresholds. Our cities seem to be losing such social forms irretrievably. We have witnessed this radical change

during the last three decades. Since the early 1960s, in the metropolitan centres of the developed world, city fabrics largely inherited
from the nineteenth century have been overlaid by the twin development of the freestanding high-rise and the serpentine freeway. This
erosion of public space, and entailed in this the effacing of cultural
memory, which always needs an architectonic prop, finds expression
in Melvin Webber's concepts of 'community without propinquity'
and the 'non-place urban realm',[76] and in Robert Venturi's assertion
that Americans do not need piazzas because they should be at home
watching television.[77]

That last remark, fatuous though it is, nevertheless yields a
further clue as to the nature of the transformation in question. This
change may be expressed by saying that an architecture of volume
is being replaced by an architecture of surface. There is an eerie
sense in which this mutation was anticipated long ago. Victor Hugo
once put into the mouth of Claude Frollo, the Archdeacon of Notre
Dame, who could still 'read' his cathedral and its surroundings as
one might read a hieroglyphic scripture, the prophecy that the book
will bring about the death of architecture; by which he meant not
ornately hand-lettered books but machine-printed books which implied the ideal of universal literacy. For, so Hugo thought, once the
mysteries could be spelt out from printed words, the desire for a built
'summa', the cathedral or the monument, would atrophy and gradually dissolve the very idea of a humanly made environment charged
with meaning.[78] But modern space is, as it were, space wiped clean.
The architectural and urbanistic space of modernity tends precisely
towards a homogeneous space, in which everything is alike, in which
marks and markers are added after the fact; all of which reinforces
a physical discomfort and a feeling of desertedness. We may even
speak of this architectural and urbanistic space of modernity as a
post-Cartesian space, at least in the sense that it is the space of blank
sheets of paper, drawing boards, plans, scale models and geometrical
proportions.[79] And, adapting Victor Hugo's anticipation, we may say
that it is not the book but the screen that will bring about the death

of architecture. This is why Venturi's remark about the piazza being superseded by the television discloses a truth behind its falsity; for all its silliness it indicates a real trend. An architecture of volume is replaced by an architecture of surface, buildings by screens, monumentality by miniaturisation. There is a sense, then, in which one of the most important features of present-day architecture is the screen on which we are presented with particles in motion, the screen where omnipresent visibility appears in the twin manifestation of news circulation and advertising copy.

A powerful source of contemporary cultural amnesia thus has to do with the nature and the life history of the material objects with which people are customarily surrounded. Today, we are surrounded everywhere by the conspicuousness of consumption through the multiplication of objects and material garb. Large department stores, with an abundance of consumer goods and clothing, provide the primary landscape of affluence; our markets and our malls are, so to speak, a second nature of prodigious fecundity. The contemporary indoctrination into systematic, organised consumption is the extension, in the present, of the earlier indoctrination of rural populations into industrial labour which occurred in the nineteenth century. From the standpoint of cultural memory, it is not simply the fecundity of consumable objects, it is rather their *lifespan*, that is significant.[80] The norms of social standing impose a time-scheduling, a metabolism, of increasingly rapid cycles. As Baudrillard has said, we are now living in the period of objects; we live by their rhythm, according to their cycles. Today it is we who observe the birth and death of objects; whereas in all previous civilisations it was the object and the monument that survived the generations. Compared with all previous history, the life expectancy of people and that of buildings is now reversed. The accelerated metabolism of objects generates the attenuation of memory.

Of all potentially obsolescent objects, the sign is pre-eminent. Its rate of obsolescence seems to be nearer that of an automobile than that of a building, and, potentially, it is faster still. The reason for

this is not to be found in any process of physical deterioration intrinsic to the sign; it is to be sought, rather, in what competitors
with other signs are doing. We can learn here from Las Vegas.[81] Las
Vegas presents intensified communication along the highway. The
little low buildings, grey-brown like the desert, separate and recede
from the street that is now the highway; their fake fronts become dis-
engaged and are turned perpendicular to the highway, as huge, high
signs. The most unique, the most monumental parts of the Strip in
Las Vegas, the signs and casino facades, are also the most changeable;
it is the neutral structures behind them that survive a succession of
facelifts and a series of themes up front. As Venturi says: the sign
is more important than the architecture; if you take the sign away,
there is no place.[82]

The signs in the Strip in Las Vegas signal a cultural mutation
in the history of material objects. Of most material objects at most
times we can say that, even though they do not speak to us, we
can understand these material settings because they have meanings
which we habitually decode; or, better still, we should say that we
frequently do not consciously decode them because they seem not
to resist our capacity to decipher them. The very notion of decoding
objects as signs becomes necessary to us to the degree that there
is an inbuilt obsolescence in the world of material things. Before
this transformation in the cultural biography of things they are not
so much conceptual hieroglyphs as rather sites which we inhabit.
This is why we can learn from Las Vegas. For we can distinguish
three successive, though overlapping, cultural stages. There was
the *theory* of the arbitrariness of the linguistic sign propounded in
Saussurean structural linguistics; then, somewhat later, there was
the *application* of the theory of the arbitrariness of the sign to cultural studies generally; and then, there was the conscious accelerated *material fabrication* of systems of arbitrary signs flaunting
their sign-nature.

I have said that of all potentially obsolescent things the sign
is pre-eminent. But what if things cease to exist? Put like that the

question seems preposterous. But let us take as a definition of a thing something that can be held in the hand. The hand characteristic of the human organism grasps things; and many of the things grasped by the hand are held and manipulated so as to be transformed, whether in agrarian or in manufacturing cultures. Indeed, the idiom 'I cannot grasp this', which is employed to make emphatic our inability to understand something, is grounded in the fact that the human hand traditionally grasps things and by this means learns to handle and so control the environment; just as the idiom 'I can handle this' reassures my interlocutor that I am faced with a situation with which I can confidently cope; just as, again, the expressions 'too hot to handle' or 'playing with fire' indicate my settled belief that I am confronted with a circumstance with which I think it imprudent to get entangled. But the information that now floods the environment – perhaps it is telling that the verb we commonly use is taken from the element of water which cannot be held in the hand – displaces from our milieu the things in it that could be grasped by the hands. A computer memory or an electronic image are non-things in the sense that they cannot be held in the hand; they can only be accessed by the fingertips. Any attempt to grasp the electronic pictures on a television screen, or the data stored in computers, or reels of film or microfilm, is bound to fail. These non-things, as Vilem Flusser[83] calls them, are of course trapped within things: silicon chips, cathode-ray tubes, laser beams. But these non-things are impossible to get hold of by the hands. These non-things that proliferate all around us we call information. An ever larger proportion of humanity is engaged in the production of information, an ever smaller proportion is involved in producing things. Humanity is becoming dominated by those who have control over this type of information: the construction of atomic power stations, weapons, genetic engineering. The lack of solidity of the culture from which things are increasingly absent is becoming our daily experience. All that is solid melts into information.[84]

4

We can see, then, that these phenomena are mutually reinforcing and interlocking. The increased scale of human settlement, the production of speed, and the repeated intentional destruction of the built environment, generate a diffuse yet all-encompassing and powerful cultural amnesia; and they are in their turn generated by the capitalist process of production. Modernity, or at least that component of it represented by the economic expansion of the capitalist process of production, produces cultural amnesia not by accident but intrinsically and necessarily. Forgetting is built into the capitalist process of production itself, incorporated in the bodily experience of its life-spaces.

NOTES

1. R. S. Lopez, 'The crossroad within the wall', in O. Handlin and
   J. Burchard, eds., *The Historian and the City* (Cambridge, Mass., 1963),
   pp. 27–43.
2. P. Hohenberg and L. H. Lees, *The Making of Urban Europe, 1000–1950*
   (Cambridge, Mass., 1985), p. 51; N. J. G. Pounds, *An Historical
   Geography of Europe, 450BC–AD1330* (Cambridge, 1973). 'At a time
   when most English towns had fewer than 5,000 inhabitants, Florence and
   Milan each had over 50,000 residents ... small English market towns bore
   little resemblance to the port cities of the Mediterranean culminating
   in the imperial city, Constantinople. It is important not to reduce this
   fascinating array of places to the bland homogeneity of "the medieval
   town".' Hohenberg and Lees, *The Making of Urban Europe*, pp. 27–8.
3. Ibid., p. 51.
4. Ibid., pp. 32–3.
5. W. Braunfels, *Urban Design in Western Europe: Regime and
   Architecture, 900–1900* (Eng. tr. Chicago and London, 1988), pp. 35, 38.
6. J. de Vries, *Economy in Europe in an Age of Crisis, 1600–1750*
   (Cambridge, 1976), p. 151.
7. On new baroque capitals see J. de Vries, *European Urbanization,
   1500–1800* (London, 1984).
8. M. Girouard, *Cities and People: A Social and Architectural History*
   (New Haven, Conn., 1985) pp. 258, 344–5.

9. See the description of the cities of Flanders, especially Bruges and Ghent, by Hieronymus Münzer, in *Itinerarion sive Peregrinatio excellentissimi viri* [1495]; *Voyage aux Pays-Bas*, intr. M. Delcourt (Brussels, 1942).

10. Braunfels, *Urban Design in Western Europe*, p. 94.

11. Ibid., p. 302.

12. Ibid., p. 94.

13. Hohenberg and Lees, *The Making of Urban Europe*, pp. 305–6.

14. E. Hobsbawm, 'Labour in the great city', *New Left Review*, 166 (1987), pp. 39–52.

15. I. Katznelson, *Marxism and the City* (Oxford, 1993), p. 217.

16. R. M. Pritchard, *Housing and the Spatial Structure of the City* (Cambridge, 1976).

17. J. E. Vance, Jr, 'Housing the worker: determinative and contingent ties in nineteenth century Birmingham', *Economic Geography*, 43 (1967).

18. J. Prest, *The Industrial Revolution in Coventry* (Oxford, 1960).

19. F. Trowell, 'Speculative housing development in the suburbs of Headingley, Leeds, 1838–1914', *Publications of the Thoresby Society*, 59 (1983).

20. D. J. Olsen, 'Victorian London: specialization, segregation, and privacy', *Victorian Studies*, 17 (1974); A. S. Wohl, 'The housing of the working classes in London', in S. D. Chapman, ed., *The History of Working Class Housing: A Symposium* (Newton Abbot, 1971).

21. Katznelson, *Marxism and the City*, pp. 200–1.

22. R. Sennett, *The Conscience of the Eye: The Design and Social Life of Cities* (New York, 1990), chapter 2.

23. On this point generally see Hobsbawm, 'Labour in the great city'.

24. P. Joyce, *Work, Society, and Politics: The Culture of the Factory in Late Victorian England* (New Brunswick, 1980), stresses that the factory town of the mid to late nineteenth century 'retained more of the village than it acquired of the city. Understood as the "walking city" the factory town grew by cellular reproduction, the town slowly absorbing factory neighbourhoods in its expansion.' Until the introduction of tramways and bicycles 'the link between home and work remained firm until these severed it', pp. 118–19.

25. Katznelson, *Marxism and the City*, p. 235; P. H. J. H. Gosden, *The Friendly Societies in England* (Manchester, 1961). For the construction

of local 'mappings' in the lived spaces of the nineteenth-century city see J. A. Agnew, *Place and Politics: The Geographical Mediation of State and Society* (Boston, 1987).

26. R. Aminzade, *Class, Politics, and Early Industrial Capitalism: A Study of Mid-Nineteenth Century Toulouse* (Albany, NY, 1981).

27. M. Gottdiener, *The Social Production of Urban Space* (Austin, Tex., 1985).

28. This feature of contemporary settlement space is investigated by S. Sassen, *The Mobility of Labor and Capital: A Study of International Investment and Labor Flow* (Cambridge, 1988); D. Massey, *Spatial Division of Labor* (London, 1984); A. J. Scott, 'Flexible production systems and regional development: the rise of new industrial spaces in North America and Western Europe', *International Journal of Urban and Regional Research*, 12 (1988); P. Hall and A. Markusen, eds., *Silicon Landscapes* (Boston, 1985); N. S. Dorfman, 'Route 128: the development of a regional high technology economy', *Research Policy*, 12 (1983); M. Piore and C. Sabel, *The Second Industrial Divide* (New York, 1984); J. Urry, 'Class, space and disorganised capitalism', in K. Hoggart and E. Kofman, eds., *Politics, Geography and Social Stratification* (London, 1986).

29. R. Rogers, *Cities for a Small Planet* (London, 1997), p. 27.

30. M. Castells, *The Rise of the Network Society* (Oxford, 1996), p. 403.

31. Ibid., 403–10. 'What is most significant about megacities is that they are connected externally to global networks and to segments of their own countries, while internally disconnecting local populations that are either functionally unnecessary or socially disruptive ... this is true of New York as well as of Mexico or Jakarta. It is this distinctive feature of being globally connected and locally disconnected, physically and socially, that makes megacities a new urban form.' Ibid., p. 404.

32. K. Lynch, *The Image of the City* (Cambridge, Mass., 1960).

33. Frank Lloyd Wright, 'The Industrial Revolution runs away', *The Disappearing City* (1932), cited in K. Frampton, *Modern Architecture* (London, 1993), p. 190.

34. See P. Virilio, *Speed and Politics* (New York, 1986).

35. A. Friedberg, *Window Shopping: Cinema and the Post-Modern* (Berkeley, 1993), p. 3.

36. Ibid., pp. 82, 84, 152.

37. E. Dimendberg, 'The will to motorization: cinema, highways, and modernity', *October*, 73 (1995), p. 95.

38. Ibid., p. 107.

39. Ibid., pp. 121–2, 136–7. See D. E. Nye, *American Technological Sublime* (Cambridge, Mass., 1996).

40. J. R. Griffith, 'The complete highway: modern transportation in the light of ancient philosophy', *Landscape Architecture*, 47 (1957), p. 352.

41. Dimendberg, 'The will to motorization', p. 136.

42. Quoted in D. Harvey, *Consciousness and the Urban Experience* (Oxford, 1985), p. 15.

43. Quoted in ibid., p. 16.

44. Castells, *The Rise of the Network Society*, p. 422.

45. On displacement in contemporary Paris see N. Evenson, *Paris: A Century of Change, 1878–1978* (New Haven, Conn., 1979); for a brief account of the effects of the breakup of *arrondissements* and their cultural memories see R. Cobb, 'The assassination of Paris', *New York Review of Books* (February 1980).

46. P. Virilio and S. Lotringer, *Pure War* (New York, 1983), p. 64.

47. On the contrast between the space of places and the space of flows see M. Castells, 'High technology, economic restructuring, and urban-regional process in the United States', in M. Castells, ed., *High Technology, Space and Society* (London, 1985), pp. 11–40. R. Williams, 'Problems of the coming period', *New Left Review*, 140 (July–August 1983), pp. 7–18, examines this phenomenon from the point of view of what he calls 'mobile privatization'.

48. R. Banham, *Los Angeles: The Architecture of Four Ecologies* (London, 1971), p. 23.

49. D. Appleyard, K. Lynch and J. R. Myer, *The View from the Road* (Cambridge, Mass., 1964), p. 10.

50. U. Eco, *Travels in Hyperreality* (San Diego, 1986).

51. Rogers, *Cities for a Small Planet*, pp. 9–10.

52. Ibid., pp. 35–6.

53. J. Rykwert, 'Learning from the street', in *The Necessity of Artifice* (Oxford, 1982), pp. 105–13. On the road as a literary topos see M. M. Bakhtin, 'Forms of time and chronotope in the novel', in *The Dialogic Imagination* (Austin, Tex., 1992), pp. 120 ff.

54. Virilio, *Speed and Politics*, p. 23.

55. Ibid., p. 3.

56. Ibid., p. 4.

57. R. Barthes, in *Architecture d'aujourd'hui* no. 153 (December 1970 – January 1971), pp. 11–13.

58. M. de Certeau, 'Practices of space', in M. Blonsky, ed., *On Signs* (Oxford, 1985), pp. 129–30.

59. E. Husserl, 'The world of the living present and the constitution of the surrounding world external to the organism', in F. A. Elliston and P. McCormick, eds., *Husserl: Shorter Works* (Notre Dame, 1981), p. 249.

60. Ibid., p. 250. On Husserl on the subject of walking see E. Casey, *The Fate of Place: A Philosophical History* (Berkeley, Los Angeles and London, 1997), pp. 224–8.

61. Quoted in W. Schivelbusch, *The Railway Journey* (New York, 1979), p. 59.

62. K. Lynch, *What Time Is This Place?* (Cambridge, Mass., 1972), p. 37. 'In American cities, the urban landscape is constantly changing, as old buildings are demolished to make room for more efficient uses of their sites, as failing offices and shops are replaced by successful newcomers, as restaurants and cafés come and go. With none of the restrictive licensing still widespread in Europe and Japan, which protects old commerce by suppressing the new, with construction permits easily granted, few public institutions exempt from market forces and hardly any buildings protected by architectural preservation orders, American cities very readily adapt to shifting economic pressures, both large and very small. Overall this makes them very much more efficient as places of work and business than European cities – and much less of a home for their inhabitants. Turbo-capitalism leaves no room for emotional attachments to old buildings, old bookshops, old neighbourhood venues, or anything else for that matter. Not surprisingly, Americans are greatly attracted to such places as Paris, Rome and Kyoto, so much less adaptable and efficient than New York, Chicago or Los Angeles, so much more hospitable to human life. Parisians, Romans or even Kyoto's famously traditionalist citizens hardly lead lives of unexamined tranquillity, but among them one constantly feels that their strong sense of belonging to their cities

leaves their happiness far less dependent on the size of their disposable income.' Luttwak, *Turbo-Capitalism*, pp. 222–3.

63. Quoted in D. Harvey, *Consciousness and the Urban Experience* (Oxford, 1985), p. 28.

64. Sennett, *The Conscience of the Eye*, pp. 51–2.

65. A. Toffler, *Future Shock* (London, 1970), p. 51.

66. S. Kracauer, 'Pariser Beobachtungen', *Frankfurter Zeitung*, 13 February 1927.

67. S. Kracauer, 'Ein Paar Tagen Paris', *Frankfurter Zeitung*, 5 April 1932.

68. S. Kracauer, 'Strasse ohne Erinnerung', *Frankfurter Zeitung*, 16 December 1932.

69. Ibid.

70. S. Kracauer, 'Wiederholung', *Frankfurter Zeitung*, 29 May 1932.

71. Ibid.

72. Harvey, *Consciousness and the Urban Experience*, esp. pp. 36–7, 60–1.

73. K. Marx, *Grundrisse: Foundations of a Critique of Political Economy* (Harmondsworth, 1973), p. 538.

74. See C. Norberg-Schulz, *Existence, Space and Architecture* (London, 1971), pp. 80–6.

75. Rykwert, *The Necessity of Artifice*, pp. 131–3.

76. M. Webber, *Explorations in Urban Structure* (Philadelphia, 1964).

77. R. Venturi, *Complexity and Contradiction in Architecture* (New York, 1966), p. 133.

78. See Rykwert, *The Necessity of Artifice*, pp. 131–3.

79. See H. Lefebvre, *The Production of Space* (Oxford, 1991) esp. pp. 200 ff.

80. See J. Baudrillard, *Selected Writings*, ed. M. Poster (Oxford, 1988), pp. 29–30, and Toffler, *Future Shock*.

81. R. Venturi and D. Scott-Brown, *Learning from Las Vegas* (Cambridge, Mass., 1972). Baudrillard has also argued that Las Vegas and Los Angeles should be viewed as paradigmatic for the spaces of late capitalism, the ultimate urban form so far reached in America. See his 'Hyperreal America', *Economy and Society*, 22 (1993), pp. 243–52.

82. Venturi and Scott-Brown, *Learning from Las Vegas*, p. 12.

83. V. Flusser, *The Shape of Things: A Philosophy of Design* (Eng. tr. London, 1999), pp. 86–92.

84. As Susanne Küchler has suggested, what may now be coming to an end is the idea of memory as the conscious apprehension – the grasping – of experience through material objects and material remains; memory as a force may be shedding its material trappings on which we have so long relied. S. Küchler, 'The place of memory', in A. Forty and S. Küchler, eds., *The Art of Forgetting* (Oxford and New York, 1999), p. 54.

5   Conclusion

A number of doubts and queries will have been formed in the reader's mind with respect to the argument I have been developing. I shall now attempt to answer some of those which are foreseeable.

First of all, it may be asked, when precisely did this process of cultural forgetting emerge as a 'break' or 'rupture' to which it is possible to point as being unquestionably more important than any other? What has occurred is in fact a concatenation of 'ruptures'. To some degree, of course, my argument presupposes the classic Marxist account which places the most crucial break about 1800 onwards. But with respect to the emergence of the giant city and, a less important feature, the mass circulation of newspapers, a date about a century later, around 1900, and onwards, is a significant chronological marker. Yet again, the emergence of megacities, the increasing importance of electronic media and the development of information technology imply a date from about the middle of the twentieth century onwards, or even later still, as a significant further step-change. Overall, the process of cultural forgetting characteristic of modernity is accelerating and marked by a concatenation of step-changes.

Then again, it may be asked, where did this process of forgetting happen? My argument obviously implies that forgetting has become a problem for humanity in general, yet it is also equally clear that the process started earlier and has gone much further in some parts of the globe than in others. The answer to the question 'when?' is only possible to formulate if certain crucial differences are acknowledged. The rate at which Americans, both North and South, tear down buildings, for example, differs considerably from what Italians, or even the British, do to them.

Then again, it may be asked, to whom did this cultural forgetting happen and to whom does it now happen? There are at least four distinguishable categories of persons who experience this phenomenon on a global scale: the hegemonic group within the international division of labour; the subaltern group within the international division of labour; economic migrants; and political refugees. These are not all mutually exclusive categories; there is obviously some overlap between the last three groups.

The hegemonic group within current informational capitalism enjoys a lifestyle and moves within an environment which is increasingly homogeneous throughout the world. This ever more homogenised identity is symbolically expressed in the VIP lounges at airports, which are designed to maintain the social distance between them and all other persons using air transport; by international hotels, whose decoration, from the design of the rooms to the colour of the towels, is globally homogeneous; and in permanent access to mobile, personal, on-line telecommunications networks. These are symbols of membership in the managerial circles of the informational economy that transcends the cultural borders of nation-states throughout the world; they live within an environment and a habitus which supersede the historical specificity of each locale and therefore incline them inexorably to forget those borders.

The subaltern group are tied also to specific places, but their ties are to the particularity of local settings, rather than to a lifestyle potentially available to the hegemonic group everywhere. For the members of the subaltern group the residential area is where an interlocking network of social relationships is located. This physical area has considerable meaning to the inhabitants as an extension of the home, since various parts of it, such as pubs, convey a sense of belonging. These concrete, locally particular resources provide an experience of familiarity and stability, a sense of continuity through the memory of the locality of place. When such a neighbourhood is threatened with physical destruction, its members all band together against the threat. Throughout the late 1950s and early 1960s, the centre of the Bronx was not just threatened but destroyed, when Robert Moses planned and oversaw the construction of the Cross-Bronx Expressway where the previously 'modern' urban boulevard was blown to pieces. In *All that Is Solid Melts into Air* (1982), Marshall Berman has given a moving account of how he foresaw the fate of his neighbourhood and wept as he once stood looking at the construction site for the Cross-Bronx Expressway, and how he belonged to a group who worked to help other people, blacks, Hispanics, poor whites, Vietnamese, to fight for their own homes, even as they fled their own. These people were threatened by the attack on their memories of locality, an enforced forgetting precipitated by the repeated intentional destruction of the built environment.

The years preceding the First World War had been the greatest period of mass migration in recorded history. In the last fifteen years before 1914 almost 15 million people had landed in the United States. People also migrated from country to city and from one region of the same state to another. Almost 15 out of every 100 Poles left their country for good in the pre-First World War years. This was one reason why racism became so vehement in the late nineteenth century, leading to increasingly vociferous campaigns against mass immigration in the United States, and in Europe, where anti-Semitism was the characteristic expression of the same sentiments against migrants. Once again, during the boom years between 1945 and 1973, there was large-scale internal migration; as when Italian southerners flooded into the factories of Lombardy and Piedmont. By 1968 migrants from the Maghreb – Tunisia, Morocco and Algeria – constituted almost a quarter of all foreigners in France. Currently one-third of all immigrants in the United States come from Latin America, overwhelmingly from Central America. In the period from 1945 onwards the traumatic effects of mass migration were to some extent moderated by the segmented labour market: immigrant Jews in most western countries moved into the garment industry, and the staff of Indian restaurants in London and New York, in the 1990s, were mainly recruited from one particular district of Bangladesh.

But, as a whole, these mass migrations, both between countries and within countries, must have entailed the forgetting of local roots, even though the process would have been modified by continuing family ties in the place of origin. The history of mass migration is part of the history of modern forgetting, and of forgetting places in particular.

More traumatic still was the plight of political refugees. The First World War and the Russian Revolution forced millions to move as refugees. Between 1.5 and 2 million Russian nationals found themselves homeless after the Russian Revolution; although bearing in mind the social provenance of many of these refugees they may not all have found the question of resettlement in a new place quite as problematic as subsequent waves of refugees did; their parents might have been, for example, timber merchants with the enterprise and resourcefulness to build a new life elsewhere. Nonetheless, part of the atmosphere of the inter-war years was coloured by the fact that the period between 1914 and 1922 generated roughly between 4 and 5 million political refugees. The collapse of Germany in 1945 presents a far more dramatic case. It has been estimated that by May 1945 there were about 40.5 million uprooted people in Europe, a figure which excludes non-German forced labourers and Germans fleeing in terror from the vengeance of the advancing Russian armies. About 13 million Germans were expelled from the parts of Germany annexed by Poland and the Soviet Union, from Czechoslovakia and from parts of south-eastern Europe where they had long been settled. All these people would have had, to some degree, to forget the places from which they came.

In *The Enigma of Arrival*, V. S. Naipaul has given a wry picture of himself as a young man, seen now from the hindsight of middle life, when he stayed in an Earls Court boarding house at the age of eighteen. He already knew that he wanted to be a writer. As he wandered the streets of London in 1950, 'as a writer', he 'was still looking for suitable metropolitan material'.[1] It so happened, he later realised, that in London in 1950 he was 'at the beginning of that great movement of peoples that was to take place in the second half of the twentieth century – a movement and a cultural mixing greater than the peopling of the United States'.[2] He had a small particle of this mass movement before his very eyes in his Earls Court boarding house, where there were at least ten or twelve drifters from many countries of Europe and North Africa, who were offering themselves for his inspection, people whose 'principal possessions were their stories, and their stories spilled easily out of them'.[3] But Naipaul at eighteen could neither hear nor see this. When the stories spilled out of the displaced persons, he 'noted nothing down. He asked no questions', although he 'had found, if only I had had the eyes to see, a great subject'.[4] 'The flotsam of Europe, not long after the end of the terrible war, in a London house':[5] that, he later realised, 'was the true material of the boarding house'.[6] 'There was a subject here that could have been my own', he concludes, but at the time he was oblivious of it. And so, looking back on his eighteen-year-old self, he concludes that he 'had little to record'.[7] The people he saw were full of their memories, which he did not record; later, as political refugees who had forcibly to resettle in another country, they themselves would slowly forget at least some things about their places of origin.

A further question might be posed in response to my argument that the modern production of spaces tends to generate cultural amnesia. For have there not been movements of resistance, of concerted opposition, to the enormous mutation of the human habitat generated by the changed scale of emplacement, the production of speed, and the repeated intentional destruction of the built environment? There have in fact been significant resistances. There was the resistance of topographical inertia, and there was the resistance occasioned by human intervention.

The resistance of inertia results from the fact that nothing is less flexible than the urban street layout. The housing system, as distinct from individual houses, is a force which makes for a massive permanence in the life of a city. The urban street plan is particularly resistant to change, such that it is possible to study the persistence of a city's layout, as laid down in the plan of its streets, much as one might investigate a genealogical network.

The persistence brought about by human intervention can take a variety of forms. I cite two examples only, one taken from France in the early twentieth century, the other from England in the late twentieth century.

Between 1900 and 1920 Atget assembled an enormous photographic archive of Parisian artefacts dating from the *Ancien Régime* to the mid nineteenth century. He was reacting to the enormous topographical transformation of Paris since the mid nineteenth century, which had proceeded in two phases. In the first phase, under Haussmann, twenty-two new boulevards were begun, avenues such as Lafayette, Rivoli and Kléber were constructed, and the Solferino, Alma and Change bridges were built across the Seine. These vast new designs required the destruction of many existing structures, particularly in the Latin Quarter and the Île de la Cité. Then, in a second phase, between 1892 and 1902, 171 new streets were constructed; the western extension to the Rue Réaumur on the Right Bank from Saint-Denis to Notre-Dame-des-Victoires was established in 1895–6; the Rue du Louvre was linked at its northern end with the Rue Montmartre in 1906; and the Boulevard Raspail was joined to the Rue Montparnasse in 1890. These changes, once again, meant the sacrifice of existing structures, as when sections of the 1st arrondissement, especially the Rue des Deux-Écus, were demolished in 1907.

These vast transformations provoked a counter-movement. Between 1890 and 1895, de Champeaux produced a detailed series of illustrated articles on the decorative ornamentation of old Parisian architecture in the *Gazette des Beaux-Arts*; in 1903 the Marquis de Rochegude's *Guide à travers le vieux Paris* appeared; and in November 1897 an official body, the Commission municipale du vieux Paris, was established to resist the persistent destructions. Atget's photographic archive is situated within this movement of resistance to the new place-world of Paris at the opening of the twentieth century. The invention of photography formed a cultural counter-weight to the invention of railways; the latter produced speed, the former created stillness; the latter unsettled remembering, the former gave it a new sedimentation. But it was not so much the production of speed as rather the repeated destruction and restructuring of the built environment that most preoccupied Atget, and against which he fought a kind of rearguard cultural campaign for twenty years.

He avoided all those monuments which were much photographed at the time, such as the Louvre, the Sainte-Chapelle and the Tour Saint-Jacques. He never took as a photographic subject the most photographed piece of Parisian topography after 1889: the Eiffel Tower. Amidst thousands of photographs, it appears once only, and then, as is evident from the photograph, almost certainly inadvertently; it appears in a photograph he took around 1901 of Passy, Rue Barton, and can be discerned only in the distance, in miniature, and through a haze.

Atget's archive is of the premodern city, both its places and its people. He photographed old streets, old courtyards, the interiors of shops, bars, markets, junk shops, horse-drawn tramways, carriages and wagons, fountains, bridges, barges, churches, doorknobs. He also photographed the street commerce that was archaic: flower-sellers, rag-pickers, street musicians, garbage collectors, prostitutes, beggars and tramps. He turned the artefactual remains of the *Ancien Régime* into a vast photographic archive.

More recently, the heritage industry in England has produced some sensible and many bizarre attempts to counteract the modern construction of space and the repeated intentional destruction of the built environment. English Heritage, founded in 1984 to take charge of historic buildings and monuments, had by the mid 1990s some 500,000 properties for which it was responsible, among them an entire town, the lead-mining district of Derbyshire, Wirksworth. The number of listed ancient monuments was 268 in 1882, 12,900 by 1994. In towns, cobblestones were routinely incorporated during the 1980s within the repertoire of what municipal authorities termed 'environmental improvement', making no-go areas for the motorist, and returning previously dilapidated streets to what Kensington Council referred to as 'Victorian grandeur'. In the country, 'Heritage Walks' and 'Heritage Trails' were taken up by municipal authorities to mark the European Architectural Heritage Year in 1975 and the celebration of the Silver Jubilee in 1977.

The virtual disappearance of manufacturing industry and the near disappearance of heavy manual labour prompted into life the practice of 'industrial archaeology', a term coined in 1953, to protect abandoned or salvaged industrial plant. Initially the most numerous type of industrial monument was the windmill and watermill; the Society for the Protection of Ancient Buildings publishes a list of 180 mills open to the public in England. The most frequented industrial monument is the memorial to the steam railway, thirty-four of which attract 2,800,000 passengers yearly. There are at least seventeen railway museums or railway centres attracting not far short of 2 million visitors annually. The notion of a 'historic' monument has been enlarged to include Victorian public utilities like the Abbey Mills sewage works. By 1971 it was feasible to publish a coffee-table book entitled *Our Grimy Heritage*, 'a fully illustrated study of the factory chimney in Britain'.[8] At Wigan Pier Heritage Centre, you can pay to crawl through a model coal mine, and be invited in by actors and actresses dressed as 1900 proletarians.

Finally, it may be asked: what, precisely, is forgotten? To answer this question we need to distinguish between different categories of remembering; specifically, between cognitive memories, personal memories and habitual memories.

Cognitive memory claims to cover those uses of the verb 'to remember' when we may be said to remember, for example, the meaning of words, or lines of verse, or stories, or truths of logic. Applied to places, a failure of cognitive memory could mean, for example, the inability to recall the gestalt of a city, the memory of an overall shape which is indispensable if we are to be able to orient ourselves in that city. To forget the variegated street layout of a large city might entail a whole host of forgettings: of landmarks, pathways, street intersections, as well as the often complicated structure of subway systems which form a parallel geographical system beneath ground level.

By comparison with modern settlements, the spatial memorability of the early modern European habitat was grounded in their small scale, which was in turn reinforced by two features: the perimeter, that easily recognisable, and therefore cognitively memorable, outline of fortifications, gates and towers and heavy stone walls; and their point of central focus, which in European cultures was provided by those Gothic cathedrals that yielded a memorable figure against the ground of the surrounding topography. The habitat of the modern city, by contrast, became ever more boundless. With the symbolic dismantling of city walls in the nineteenth century, the emerging modern city developed endlessly and its history became a story of spatial dispersal. When populations are distributed over ever expanding regions, both massive in scope and amorphous in form, the city becomes ever less a memorable physical entity that might yield a point of focus. The disappearance of the radiocentric city generates a mode of emplacement that is more easily forgettable.

Personal memories, as distinct from cognitive memories, entail a class of personal memory claims which refer to those acts of remembering that take as their object one's own life history. We speak of them as personal memories because they are located in and refer to a personal past; through personal memory claims, persons have a special access to facts about their own past histories, a mode of access that, in principle, they can never have to the past histories of other persons. My personal memory claims may be expressed in the form of statements such as: I did this and that, at such and such a time, in such and such a place. In remembering an event, I am also reflecting upon myself. When I say 'I first visited Rome twenty years ago', I am reflecting about myself as well as about Rome. I am aware of my actual present, and I am also reflecting upon myself as the person who did this and that in the past, at such and such a place. I, who first visited Rome twenty years ago, and I, who now speak about that past event in my life, are in some senses different and in some senses identical. Personal memory claims of this kind are critical to my self-description, because my past history is a rich resource for my conception of myself; my self-knowledge, my view of my character and potentialities, is to a large degree determined by the way in which I view my own past actions. All these past actions were located somewhere. There is a vital connection between my personal identity and a variety of backward-looking states, of pleasure, of remorse, of regret; the appropriate objects of pleasure or remorse or regret are my past actions or omissions. When applied to failures of remembering, a person who recalled only imprecisely a visit to the Prado, which they made ten years previously, would demonstrate the fact that this particular occasion in their life history left little personal impact upon them, that it in no way could be said to have been a deeply assimilated experience, and that, in consequence, it no longer nurtures, or perhaps never did nurture, their personal life.

There is a further set of memory claims distinguishable from both personal memory claims and from cognitive memory claims. These are habit memories, which consist in our having the capacity to reproduce proficiently a certain set of performative acts. We remember how to read or write or swim or ride a bicycle or how to behave at a convivial meal in appropriate ways; in all of these cases it is a matter of our being able to do these things effectively when the occasion arises. We frequently do not remember how or when or where we acquired this particular type of knowledge, of knowing and remembering how to read or write or swim or ride a bicycle or behave appropriately at table; often it is only by the fact of the performance that we are able to exemplify to others the fact that we do in fact remember these things. The meaning of how to read or write or swim or ride a bicycle or eat at table is, as Bergson observed, like the meaning of a lesson thoroughly learned. It has all the characteristics of a habit, for it has been fully incorporated into my bodily performances, and the better I remember this class of habit memories the less likely it is that I shall recall some particular occasion on which I learned the matter in question; it is only when I find myself in difficulties that I may turn to my recollection, to my voluntary memory, as a guide. Applied to failures of remembering, a person who forgot their manners at table would exemplify the fact that they had only insufficiently incorporated a culturally specific manner of appropriate behaviour at table.

With specific reference to place, what can be forgotten, in addition to the cognitive forgetting of a spatial layout, the landmarks, the entrances and exits, the pathways of a human settlement, may be a set of personal memories and of habit memories. Under the conditions of modernity and the places characteristic of it, in addition to a range of cognitive memories, a particularly powerful interweaving of personal memories and habit memories, as they form layers of reciprocally reinforcing meanings, is lost.

The process of producing objects can generate cultural forgetting because if you live in a large city you may produce artefacts or services and consume goods in a market which, in reality, has extensive linkages to people and to places that remain invisible to you, unknown to you, perhaps unimagined by you. You may be unaware of these linkages, in which case you are ignorant. Or you may know about them with a greater or lesser degree of precision, but in the ongoing process of your daily life you might edit them out of the sphere of your conscious preoccupations, in which case you will forget about them; the relationships in which the flow of merchandise is enmeshed will be obscured from your view. This is primarily a cognitive forgetting, in the sense that you may have the culturally reinforced mental habit of forgetting, for example, that what you refer to as 'the countryside' or 'the landscape' are places where a labour of production by other groups of persons goes on daily in a milieu represented, and partly misrepresented, by the terms 'the countryside' or 'the landscape'.

Consumer objects now characterise to an increasing extent the life quality of human emplacement in the materially most advanced centres of the world, where the scarcity and impoverishment of vast tracts and many groups throughout the world are for the most part forgotten, a mental habit of forgetting generated by the taken-for-grantedness of consumer-availability in the metropolis. Once capitalist entrepreneurs turned their attention systematically from the production of consumer durables to the production of consumer services, the 'product life cycle' of consumable objects became ever shorter, and social distinctions were displayed by ever smaller time differences in the acts of consuming objects. A ranking system of consumable objects, which organises rapid turnover, affects both children and adults: children, who acquire an early training in the meaning of obsolescence; and adults, who are constrained by the velocity of fashion since what is fashionable disappears as rapidly as it appears. The decreasing lifespan of consumer objects precipitates an ironic cultural reversal. The life expectancy of persons increases while the life expectancy of artefacts, of objects and of buildings, decreases; as the former enjoy greater longevity, the latter are characterised by ever greater brevity. This generates a cultural forgetting of both personal and habit memories.

The production of modern information is so organised that the principles of journalistic reportage – apparent novelty, brevity, disconnection between discrete items which might, in fact, be interconnected in complex ways – isolates what has happened from the private sphere where it might earlier have entered more deeply, and so more memorably, into the effective life of persons. This generates a cultural forgetting of items of information; that also has consequences for the culturally predominant features of affective life and for the culturally predominant habits of perception, and in that sense the forgetting pertains to both personal memories and habitual memories. These forms of forgetting are potentiated by the fact that one of the most important features of contemporary topography is the miniaturised architecture of the screen, where the visibility of particles in motion signals the circulation of news and of advertising copy. For the telespectator even the most immediate past becomes an evanescent accumulation of images the transmission of which weakens the links between items, and therefore the memory of them; but it also weakens the linkages within personal experience, where pieces of information might formerly have had greater chance of 'settling down', and so becoming memorable. Information technology, by projecting 'memory' outside persons, divests personal memory of many of its former assimilative roles; by directing the attention of those addicted to its immense capacities of storage and material, and to a rapid succession of micro-events, it generates a culturally induced mental habit which makes it increasingly difficult to envision even the short-term past as 'real'; both the velocity and the disconnectedness of the items of information conveyed shape a habit of forgetting even the most recent past.

The pace of diffusion of late twentieth-century and early twenty-first-century technologies, like computers, is so much faster than that of nineteenth-century technologies, like electricity, that casual labour markets are institutionalised and temporary work contracts are increasingly pervasive. The effect of this is that the memory of habitual skills is devalued, and might as well be forgotten, while personal memories are devalued too, when the possibilities of a life 'career' become increasingly variable, and the horizon of the past shrinks for the former professional as well as for the blue-collar worker. This affects the longevity of both habit memories and personal memories. The impact of this process on the experience of places is dramatic. Large corporations view investment in particular places increasingly as a short-term matter, so that the memories of local identity on the part of subaltern groups are more and more threatened. That in turn erodes cultural trust, on the part of employees or potential employees, since trust needs a history, a past, as its matrix. The link between a person and their work, one of the most important threads in the network of personal remembering, is effaced and increasingly forgotten. In the materially most advanced areas of the world the increasing life expectancy of persons is undercut by the decreasing life expectancy of their careers. More and more, the latter might as well be forgotten.

A culture of mechanical reproduction produces memory differently from the way it was produced when earlier writing systems predominated. The culture of writing yielded a metaphorical harvest: the metaphors of writing as 'trace', as a 'sign' of a lost presence, which nonetheless remains present before the eyes, available, for reflective scrutiny; together with the idea of the 'engraving' upon our minds of lasting 'impressions', of 'background', of 'depth', and of a 'layering' of meanings. Current electronic communication will increasingly render such metaphors archaic, because the cascade of images they generate can less plausibly be claimed to engender a form of 'engraving', an active mode of remembering. It is intrinsic to the politics of memory pursued by those exercising control within the system of commercialised communication that the images purveyed will lead not to a high valuation being attached nor to the act of remembering, but to the ability to discard, and to the production of images whose seriality intensifies forgetting. This is culturally significant because whenever it can be said with precision that a person 'recollects', that recollection refers back to the person who is engaged in the activity of remembering. Every remembered person or place or idea or artefact refers back – implicitly, if not explicitly – to the person who remembers. Contemporary media weaken the threats of that specific reference, and so diminish personal memory as a cultural value.

The condition of the nineteenth-century urban proletariat, uncertain about employment and lodging, generated within the city a great uprooting, a massive rupture between persons and places; and this long-range historical uprooting was subsequently affected by the production of speed. The conquest over the tyranny of distance, and the tendential supersession of particular locatedness, brought with it both the euphoria of the momentary and the often enforced forgetting of locatedness in a specific place. When mechanisation generated accelerated mobility it also undermined the assumption that what was visual was also stable; what was seen acquired a quality of evanescence, making both personal memories and habit memories more and more forgettable, because they had less opportunity of becoming culturally sedimented.

Even if this is conceded, it might be objected, nevertheless, that intensified archivalisation leads not to cultural forgetting, but to an *excess* of cultural memory. The new carriers of 'data' make possible processes of sorting 'information' and seeking for information which are administered on an ever more exhaustive and efficient basis. Mountains of archivalised photographs, of tape-recording, of videos, increase all the time, even though they are more fragile, with respect to their stability over long time sequences, when compared with the printed word. But we now live in such an 'over-informed' culture that cleverness will consist, not in accumulating information, which today can be done by any child on the internet, but in rejecting information. The inextricable mixture of art, the market and the mass media leads to a situation in which it becomes more and more difficult for those who are creative to be 'forgetful'. The radio, the press and television are continually producing a chaotic reprise of a comprehensive archival deposit.

This suggests a paradox. The virtually interminable production of books and articles on cultural memory, when graphed chronologically, resembles over the past twenty years and more a steadily mounting fever of preoccupation which might be said to resemble the rising physical fever of a hospital patient whose condition is registered on a medical chart. In this sense, as well as because of our currently pervasive archivalisation, we are living in a culture of hypermnesia.

Yet if we examine the structures of time which systematically pattern the contemporary political economy – the temporalities of consumption, of working careers, of information production, and the production of modern spaces – we are led to the seemingly opposite conclusion, namely, that we are living in a post-mnemonic, a forgetful, culture.

Both conclusions are correct. The paradox of a culture which manifests so many symptoms of *hypermnesia* and which yet at the same time is *post-mnemonic* is a paradox that is resolvable once we see the causal relationship between these two features. Our world is hypermnesic in many of its cultural manifestations, and post-mnemonic in the structures of the political economy. The cultural symptoms of hypermnesia are caused by a political-economic system which systemically generates a post-mnemonic culture – a modernity which forgets.

NOTES

1. V. S. Naipaul, *The Enigma of Arrival* (London, 1987), p. 130.
2. Ibid., p. 240.
3. Ibid., p. 130.
4. Ibid., p. 240.
5. Ibid., p. 130.
6. Ibid., p. 240.
7. Ibid., p. 132.
8. Walter Pickles, *Our Grimy Heritage* (Fontwell, 1971).

Index